FIRST AID, CPR & AED

In Adult, Child and Infant

Copyright © 2022 by Norkor Omaboe

All rights reserved.

No part of this book may be reproduced or used in any manner, including electronic, mechanical, photocopying, or recording, without the written permission of the copyright owner except for the use of quotations in a book review.

Cover design by Pro-Designx, editing by Darío de los Santos

Printed in the United States of America

Disclaimer: the information provided in this document is based on current protocols for providing first aid at the time of its publication. This textbook is intended solely as a guide. The author makes no guarantee as to and assumes no responsibility for the completeness and outcome of the information provided in this textbook.

Table of Contents

Dedication.....12

Chapter 1

Checking the Scene.....13

Learning Objectives: - 13
Barriers To Taking Action - 15
Providing Care Until Help Arrives - 17

Chapter 2

Before Giving Care Check-Call-Care Action Steps.....19

Introduction - 19
Learning Objectives: - 19
Emergency Action Steps (Check-Call-Care) - 20

Chapter 3

Pathogens.....25

Introduction - 25
Learning Objectives - 25
Pathogens - 25
Modes Of Transmission - 26

Chapter 4 — Checking The Person.....31

Introduction - 31
Learning Objectives: - 31
Checking For Consciousness - 32
Checking A Conscious Person - 37

Chapter 5 — Cardiac Emergencies.....40

Introduction - 40
Learning Objectives - 40
 Signs Of A Heart Attack - 41
Signs And Symptoms Of A Heart Attack - 41
Signs Of A Heart Attack In Women - 42
Care For A Heart Attack - 43
Cpr - 44

Skills Review.....49

Giving Cpr To An Adult Or Child - 49

Chapter 6 — Breathing Emergencies.....58

Introduction - 58
Learning Objectives - 58
Causes Of Respiratory Distress And Respiratory Arrest - 59
Signs Of Respiratory Distress And Arrest In Adults - 60
Signs Of Respiratory Distress In Children - 60

Signs Of Respiratory Arrest In Children - 60

Care For Respiratory Distress And Respiratory Arrest - 61

Asthma - 62

Choking - 64

Care For Conscious Choking – Adults And Child - 65

Care For Conscious Choking – Infants - 68

Care For Unconscious Choking- Adult And Child - 69

Care For Unconscious Choking - Infant - 70

Preventing Breathing Emergencies In Children And Infants - 72

Skills Review.....74

Caring For An Adult Who Is Choking - 74

Caring For An Infant Who Is Choking - 78

Chapter 7 Bleeding And Shock.....80

Introduction - 80

Learning Objectives - 80

Blood And Blood Vessels - 81

Care For Minor External Bleeding - 82

Care For Severe External Bleeding - 83

Care For Internal Bleeding - 84

Using A Manufactured Tourniquet - 85

Impaled Object - 87

Shock - 87

Skills Review.....89

Using Direct Pressure To Control External Bleeding - 89

Chapter 8 — Soft Tissue Injuries
Open And Closed Wounds, Burns.....91

Introduction - 91
Learning Objectives - 91
Open Wounds - 92
Care For Amputation - 93
Penetration And Embedded Object - 94
General Care For Minor Open Wounds - 95
Care For Cheek Injuries - 95
Care For Eye Injuries - 96
Care For Nose Bleed - 96
Infections - 97
Signs Of Infection - 97
General Care For Major Open Wounds - 97
Closed Wounds - 99
Burns - 100
Lightning - 104

Chapter 9 — Musculoskeletal Injuries
Injuries To The Muscles And Bones.....106

Introduction - 106
Learning Objectives - 106
Fractures - 109
Care For Head, Neck, And Spine Injuries - 109
Sprains - 112
Strains - 114

Care For Musculoskeletal Injuries - 116

Chapter 10 — Splinting.....119

Introduction - 119
Learning Objectives - 119
General Rules For Splinting - 119
Types Of Splints - 120

Chapter 11 — Sudden Illnesses.....124

Introduction - 124
Learning Objectives - 124
General Care For Sudden Illnesses - 125
Care For Fainting - 125
Diabetic Emergency - 126
Signs Of Diabetic Emergency - 127
Care For Diabetic Emergencies - 129
Care For Seizures - 131
Stroke - 132
Signs Of A Stroke - 132
Care For A Stroke - 133
General Care For Poisoning - 134
Allergic Reactions - 135
Signs Of Anaphylaxis - 135
General Care For Allergic Reaction - 135
Care For Bee Stings - 136

Chapter 12 — Heat And Cold-Related Emergencies.....138

Introduction - 138
Learning Objectives - 138
Heat-Related Emergencies - 139
Signs Of Dehydration - 139
Care For Dehydration - 140
Heat Cramps - 140
Care For Heat Cramps - 142
Heat Exhaustion - 142
Care For Heat Exhaustion - 142
Heat Strokes - 143
Care For Heat Stroke - 143
Cold-Related Emergencies - 144
Care For Frostbites - 144
Care For Hypothermia - 146

Chapter 13 — Emergency Childbirth.....147

Introduction - 147
Learning Objectives - 147
Stages Of Labor - 148
Emergency Delivery Assistance - 149
Caring For The Newborn And The Mother - 154
Complications During Delivery - 155

Chapter 14 — Water-Related Emergencies.....157

Introduction - 157
Learning Objectives - 157
Signs Of A Water-Related Emergency - 158
General Help For Water-Related Emergencies - 159
Care For Responsive Person - 162

DEDICATION

To my dear friend, Dr. Janice Nolan, for knowing what it is like to stay up until 2:00 A. M. night after night to review this manuscript.

CHAPTER

CHECKING THE SCENE

This chapter describes the steps you should take before you step into action in an emergency. You will learn about the barriers that may prevent you from providing help, how to recognize different types of emergencies, and how to protect yourself from potential lawsuits.

LEARNING OBJECTIVES:

After reading this chapter, you will be able to:

- Understand the different types of emergencies
- Know how to overcome barriers to taking action
- Recognize the signs of an emergency
- Give care until help arrives

EMERGENCY

An emergency is a situation requiring immediate attention as a result of an accident or sudden illness. A sudden illness is a chronic or acute condition, such as a stroke or fainting. Emergencies can be life-threatening or non-life-threatening.

A **life-threatening** emergency refers to a situation in which oxygenated blood cannot reach all parts of the body. This occurs when there is a large amount of blood loss, a blocked artery, or internal bleeding. This situation requires immediate advanced medical care, and every minute counts.

A **non-life-threatening** emergency is a situation that can become life-threatening if not taken care of and therefore needs to be addressed right away. As a lay responder, you will learn to recognize an emergency and determine if the emergency is life-threatening or non-life-threatening.

SIGNS OF EMERGENCIES

Before stepping into action to help someone, your safety is the most important thing. Signs of an emergency can give clues on the nature of what happened and any potential dangers involved. If the scene is not safe, ***do not*** approach the victim. Instead, call 911 right away.

You may become aware there is an emergency based on the following signs:

- Unusual Sights: fallen ladder, smoking car off the road, downed electrical wires
- Unusual Sounds: screaming, broken glass, calls for help, sudden loud noise
- Unusual Smells: gas, fumes, an odor that is stronger than usual
- Unusual Behaviors or Appearances: slurred speech, unsteady walk, confusion, unconsciousness, trouble breathing, sudden collapse, unusual skin color

YOUR ROLE AS A LAY RESPONDER

Once you recognize an emergency, you must decide if it is safe to step into action, and what to do. We refer to these as "barriers" to taking action.

BARRIERS TO TAKING ACTION

There are several reasons people are sometimes reluctant to provide help:

NOT SURE WHAT TO DO

If you have not been trained in first aid or CPR, chances are you may panic, or simply not know what to do.

FEAR OF MAKING THE SITUATION WORSE

It is not uncommon for people to feel overwhelmed or panic. Practicing the skills outlined in this book repeatedly will help you feel confident about knowing what steps to take in the event of an emergency. The worst thing that can happen is to do nothing. If you panic or forget what to do, call 911 immediately.

UNCOMFORTABLE WITH THE SIGHT OF AN INJURY

During an emergency there can be blood, vomit, screaming, or even unpleasant odors and deformed limbs. Taking a few deep breaths before stepping into action can help you stay calm.

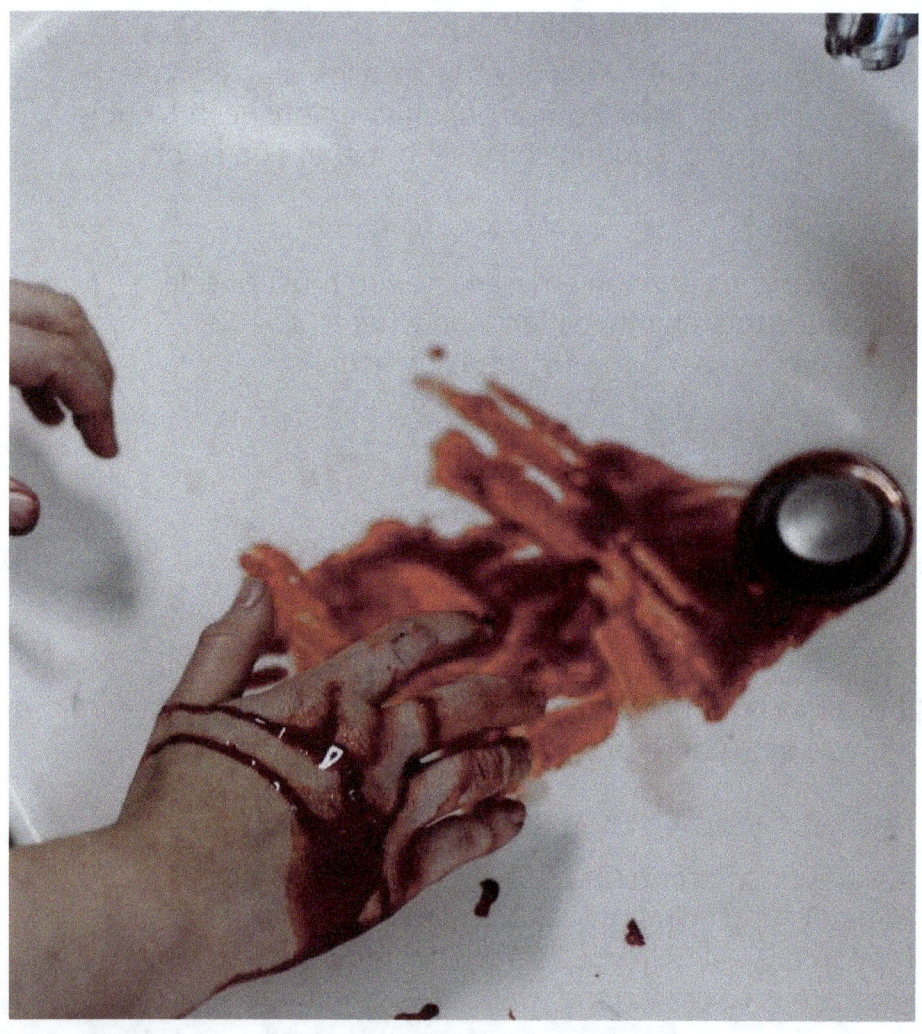

ASSUMING SOMEONE ELSE WILL HELP

When a group of people are standing around an injured victim, it is not unusual to assume someone has already called 911. If you see others giving care, you can always ask if they need your help. If no one is helping the injured victim, instruct a specific person to call the ambulance, ask one or more others to go meet and direct the ambulance to the site of the emergency, or send them to get anything you may need such as water, a sugary drink, blanket or an AED.

AFRAID OF CONTRACTING A DISEASE

It is possible to contract a disease while providing care. However, this course will teach you how diseases are transmitted, and the steps to take to protect yourself or the victims from contracting and spreading diseases.

FEAR OF BEING SUED

People are sometimes concerned about being sued for trying to help, so they prefer not doing anything. However, most lawsuits of this nature are rarely successful, as long as you follow the legal considerations outlined in the **Good Samaritan Law** (found later in this textbook).

Once you complete this textbook, you will have the confidence to step into action and use your skills to help someone.

PROVIDING CARE UNTIL HELP ARRIVES

As a lay responder, you must follow the steps outlined below every time you provide help in order to protect yourself from being sued:

Once you start helping someone, you must continue giving care to an ill or injured person unless one of the following situations occur:

- The injured or ill person asks you to stop
- You are giving CPR, and the person starts breathing on their own
- Someone as qualified as you or more qualified takes over
- The scene becomes unsafe
- You are too tired to continue.

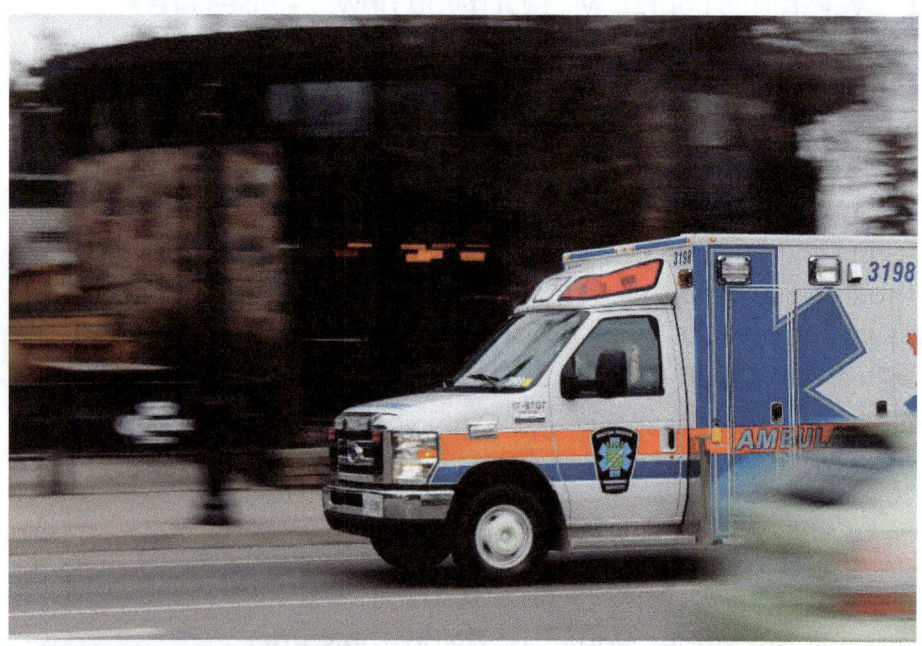

Remember, you must always ensure your own physical and legal protection before stepping into action. In the following chapter, you will learn how to apply the three action steps to use in every situation.

CHAPTER

BEFORE GIVING CARE CHECK-CALL-CARE ACTION STEPS

INTRODUCTION

In this chapter, you will learn the three action steps you must always take before giving care to an ill or injured person. You will discover 1) how to check if the situation is safe for you to proceed, 2) how to check the person, and 3) when to call 911, and 4) how to care for the person.

These three action steps are referred to as the emergency action steps and must be followed every time there is an emergency.

LEARNING OBJECTIVES:

After reading this chapter, you will be able to:

- Identify the three emergency action steps
- Determine when the scene is not safe to proceed
- Check a person for consciousness

- Describe the characteristics of life-threatening conditions

EMERGENCY ACTION STEPS (Check-Call-Care)

CHECK THE SCENE

First, you need to check the scene and look at your surroundings, ensuring it is safe for you to proceed. More specifically, check the following:

Is there an immediate danger, such as an injured person in the middle of the road? Look around and use your senses to notice if there might be smoke, electrical wires, fire, spilled chemicals, traffic, or an injured person in the water. If danger is involved, do not proceed. Instead, call 911 immediately.

Moving the Person

As a general rule, you never want to move an ill or injured person unless they are in immediate danger. If a motorcyclist is found in the middle of the road, you may need to move the person to keep you and the injured person safe. Another example is if you have to perform CPR, the person must to be on a firm surface. They will need to be moved if they are sitting behind the wheel of a car or in bed.

What Happened?

Look at clues about what may have happened. You can also ask bystanders if they have information about the situation.

Who Is Involved?

Focusing on an injured person who is screaming might be obvious, and you may not see everybody. Instead, take a moment to look around for unconscious people. If more than one person is involved, care for the most injured person first. You may have to move the lesser injured person to another person to give care.

Who Can Help?

Ask bystanders if they know the person; the able to give you some background information about their medical condition. In addition, other bystanders may have been on the scene before you and saw what happened.

On you decide to step into action, use bystanders for help. They can call 911, direct the ambulance, or help provide care.

CHECK THE PERSON

As you approach the person, look from head to toe for signs of injuries and bleeding. Next, check for consciousness. If the person is conscious, they may be able to tell you what happened. Ask them if they want you to call 911. If they do not want an ambulance, keep giving care without calling an ambulance. It is essential to understand that you must obtain consent to call an ambulance unless the person is not alert or unconscious. In that case, you have implied consent.

If the person is lying and not responding, they may be unconscious. Unconsciousness is a life-threatening condition that needs immediate action. If you are not sure if the person is conscious or not, follow these steps:

- Tap on the shoulder and ask:" Are you OK?" Speak clearly and loud. With an infant, flick the bottom of the foot to get a reaction.
- If there is no answer or reaction, have someone call 911 immediately.
- Also, use your senses to see if anything about the person is unusual, such as skin discoloration, severe bleeding, strange odor, or a bruise.

You will learn more about how to check for responsiveness in chapter 5.

A life-threatening situation includes:

- Unconsciousness
- Problem breathing
- No breathing
- Severe bleeding

CALL

Call the emergency in the following situations:

- Unconsciousness
- Problem breathing
- No breathing
- Severe bleeding
- Confusion
- Severe burn
- Vomiting blood
- Deformed limbs
- Chest pain that radiates through the arm
- Any other life-threatening condition you may encounter

If there are bystanders, have them make the call while you provide care. Ensure you point at one person specifically when asking to call the emergency; otherwise, people may expect someone else to call. Have this person stay where you are so that you are sure they made the call. When you call the emergency, provide as much information as possible; do not hang up until being told so by the dispatcher.

If you are alone, call first for all suspected cardiac emergencies. Cardiac emergencies include an unconscious adult or child 12 years old or older and a sudden collapse of a child under 12 years old.

CARE

- After checking the scene and the person, decide whether to call 911. (Remember that you can only call 911 if the person gives you consent or is unconscious or has an altered level of consciousness.).

- Obtain consent (this will be covered in chapter 3).
- If there is more than one person who is injured, give care to the person in most serious need (care for life-threatening conditions first).
- Reassure the person.
- Keep the person in the most comfortable position. Do not ask them to try to move if it hurts.
- Monitor the person's level of consciousness. For example, notice if they are breathing with more difficulty, if their skin color becomes pale, or if the person starts sweating profusely.
- Give care as needed (you will learn how in the following chapters).

Transporting the Person

At times it might be necessary to transport the injured or ill person to the hospital. In this case, have someone come with you to help monitor the person. Do not transport an injured or ill person to the hospital if:

- The person's condition may worsen and become life-threatening
- Transporting the person may make the situation worse
- You have no idea what is causing the condition

CHAPTER

PATHOGENS

INTRODUCTION

In this chapter, you will learn how to protect yourself and the injured person from transmitting and spreading diseases, what you should and should not do to protect yourself legally, and how to move an injured or ill person.

LEARNING OBJECTIVES

- List and describe the four conditions that must be present for disease transmission
- Demonstrate how to remove gloves
- Demonstrate how to obtain consent
- Explain the Good Samaritan Law
- List the six situations when it is necessary to move a person

PATHOGENS

Pathogens are agents that cause diseases, such as bacteria, viruses, parasites, and fungi. They can be transmitted between objects, people, animals, and insects contaminated with a pathogen. For a pathogen to spread, there must be four conditions:

- There is the presence of a pathogen
- There is enough pathogens to cause disease
- There is an entry point such as a cut on the skin, or an opening such as the eyes, mouth, or other mucous membranes
- The person is susceptible to the pathogen

Modes of Transmission

The transmission of pathogens can be direct or indirect.

DIRECT TRANSMISSION

Direct transmission occurs when the pathogen is spread from the infected person directly into an entry site on another person. This can happen with a splash of vomit from the infected person into the eye of another person or through sexual transmission, for example.

INDIRECT TRANSMISSION

This type of transmission occurs when the pathogen goes from the infected person to an object, and then that object contaminates another person. This can happen when a lay responder is not wearing gloves and touches a soiled item containing contaminated blood, for example. Another example is through coughing or sneezing contaminated particles into the air. This happens with flu and cold viruses.

DISEASE PREVENTION

The first step in preventing disease is to follow good personal hygiene. Wash your hands before and after giving care even if there was no direct contact with the person. When washing your hands, use soap and warm water, rub your hands for at least 20 seconds, scrub your nails, rinse thoroughly using a paper towel, and turn off the faucet using a paper towel, as well.

When washing your hands:

- Wet: wet your hands thoroughly with warm water
- Lather: lather the soap on each side of your hands and fingers
- Scrub: scrub between your fingers and underneath your nails
- Rinse: rinse thoroughly
- Dry: use paper towel to dry your hands and to turn off the faucet

Handwashing

PROTECTIVE EQUIPMENT

Keep protective equipment handy in your car and at home. You should always have the following PPE items available:

PPE items include all of the following listed below:

- Disposable gloves (includes proper removal)
- Eye protection
- CPR breathing barriers
- Masks

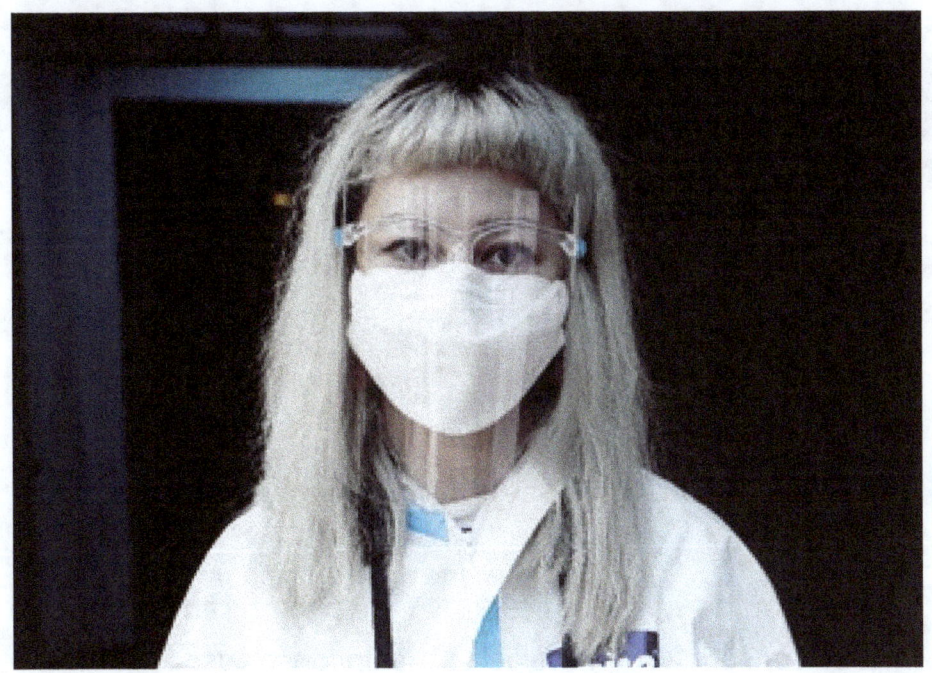
Protective goggles, gloves and mask

In addition to washing your hands, using protective equipment when giving care can protect you and the injured person. The most available equipment are disposable gloves, protective goggles, and breathing barriers. Remove rings and cover any cuts before putting your gloves on. Always wear gloves after washing your hands and before giving care. Only use disposable gloves once, and dispose of them immediately after each use. Remove them without touching bodily fluids that may have been in contact with your gloves.

Follow precautions when giving care: avoid touching your face and handling any personal items, such as keys, until you have a chance to wash your hands.

THE GOOD SAMARITAN LAW

The Good Samaritan Law protects individuals who provide first aid and CPR in an emergency if they act with the highest standards of care, have obtained consent, and do not abandon the person.

OBTAINING CONSENT

Before providing care, a lay responder must:

- Introduce him/herself
- Indicate their level of training
- Indicate what they see and what they plan on doing and
- Ask if they can help.

Consent can be verbal or gestural if the person cannot talk.

Implied consent: When the person is unconscious or unable to respond, the law may assume consent for emergency medical care. In the case of a minor, a parent or guardian must approve consent.

ABANDONMENT

Abandonment refers to the act of stopping care before it is reasonable to do so. Once you start giving care, you cannot stop unless:

- The scene becomes unsafe
- You are too exhausted to continue
- The person asks you to stop
- Someone with the same level or higher takes over.

CHAPTER 4

CHECKING THE PERSON

INTRODUCTION

So far, you have learned when it is safe to approach an injured or ill person, how to protect yourself from pathogens, how the Good Samaritan Law protects you if you act within your skills, and when to move the injured or ill person. After checking to see if the scene is safe and approaching the person, you must check for life-threatening conditions. This is the scope of this chapter.

LEARNING OBJECTIVES:

- Describe how to check for life-threatening conditions
- List and demonstrate the steps needed to check an unconscious adult, child, or infant
- Properly demonstrate how to check for breathing
- Properly demonstrate how to give two rescue breaths
- Properly demonstrate the HAINES Recovery position
- Demonstrate the SAMPLE Interview

LIFE-THREATENING CONDITIONS

There are four life-threatening conditions you need to remember:

- Problem breathing
- Absence of breathing
- Loss of consciousness
- Severe bleeding

The first step is to determine the level of consciousness. In chapter 2, you already learned how to check for consciousness. In this chapter, you'll practice and demonstrate how to check for consciousness.

After checking to see if the scene is safe, approach the person and look for signs of injuries or bleeding. If the person is conscious, they may be able to tell you what happened. Next, ask them if they want you to call 911. If they do not want an ambulance, keep giving care without calling an ambulance.

If the person is lying and not responding, they may be unconscious. Unconsciousness is a life-threatening condition that needs immediate care. If you are not sure if the person is conscious or not, follow these steps:

CHECKING FOR CONSCIOUSNESS

Tap on the shoulder and ask: "Are you OK?" Speak clear and loud. Use the person's name if you know it. Never shake an infant.

If there is no answer or reaction, have someone call 911 immediately. Also, call 911 immediately if you witness a sudden collapse of a child or infant.

Care for the person first by giving 2 minutes of care before calling 911 if a child, 12 years or younger, is unconscious but did not collapse or with a person who was drowning.

Opening the airways

An unconscious person may be breathing. Never give CPR to a breathing person, even if they are unconscious. First, open the airways to allow air to move freely. Use the head-tilt Chin-lift technique to open the airways and see if there is any sign of breathing. This technique moves the tongue from the throat, allowing air to move freely to the lungs. This step is crucial because you do not want to give CPR to a breathing person.

Head-Tilt Chin Lift Technique

- Place one hand on the injured person's forehead
- Place one or two fingers of your other hand underneath the chin of the injured or ill person
- Using both hands, gently tilt the head back to open the airways

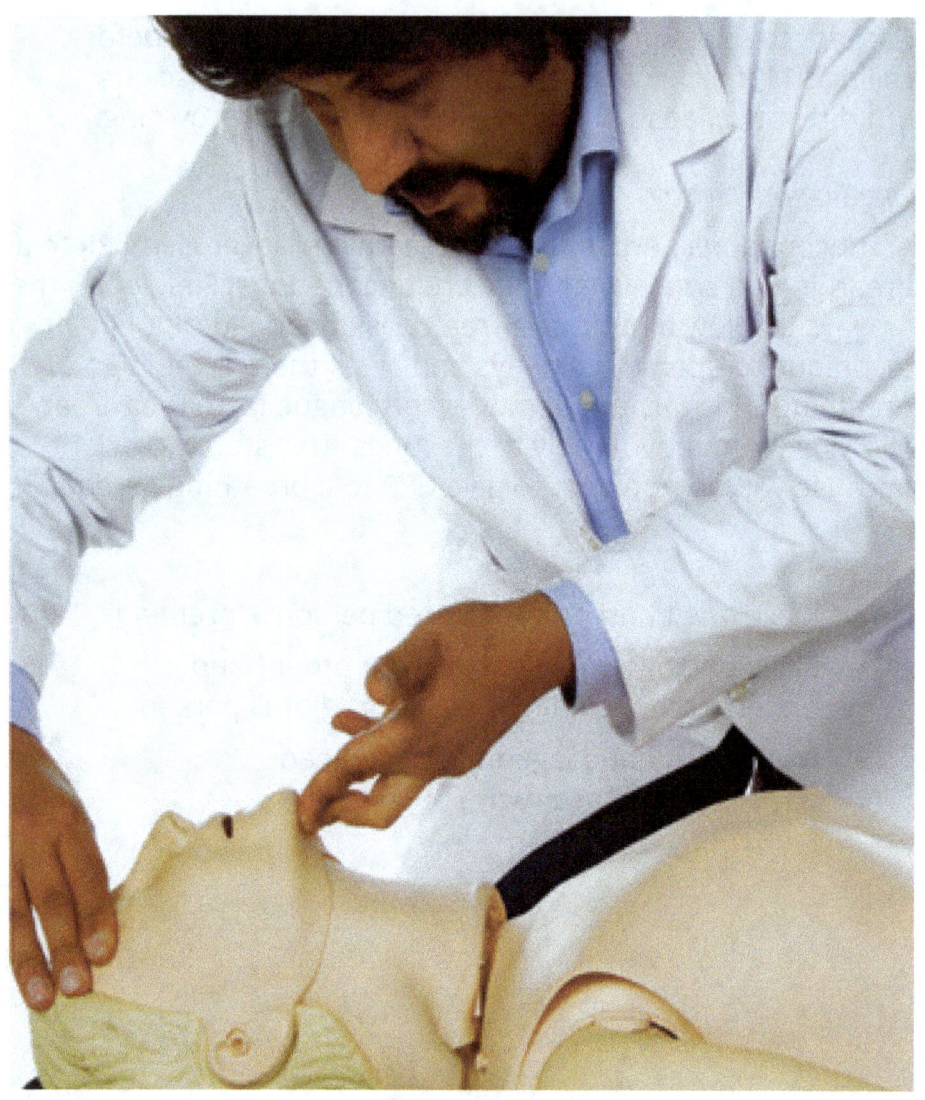

Head-tilt Chin-lift Technique

Check for Breathing (for no more than 10 seconds)

Once you've opened the airways, you must check if the unconscious person is breathing. Follow the Look, Listen, Feel steps to see, hear or feel signs of breathing:

While keeping the airways open, position yourself next to the injured or ill person, and face towards their feet. Look for the chest to rise as a sign of breathing, listen for a breathing sound coming out of the nose or mouth, and feel if air is coming out of the nose or mouth.

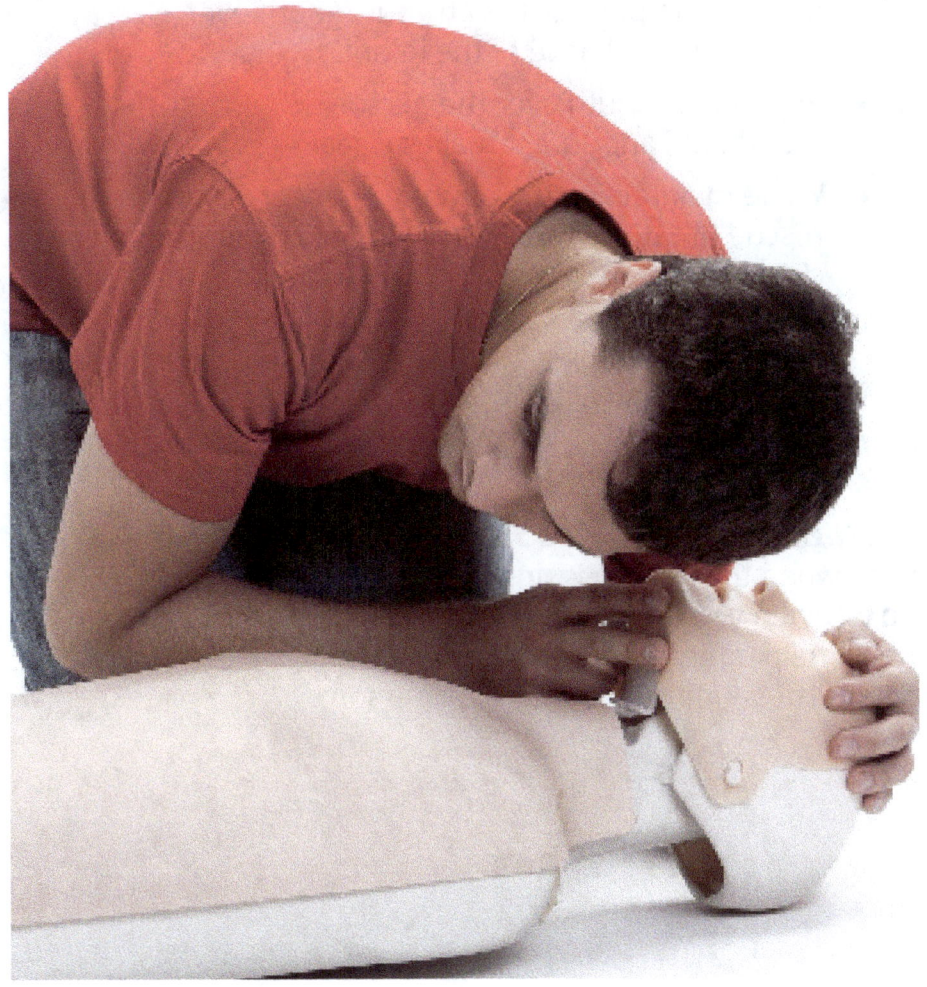

Look, listen, feel

An object or food sometimes gets stuck in the throat, preventing normal breathing. If you see something, swipe the food or object out of the mouth using your index finger.

Give Rescue Breaths
- Use a breathing barrier.
- Pinch the nose (adult and child); for an infant, make a complete seal with your mouth over the mouth and nose of the infant.
- Place your mouth over the person's mouth, making sure it makes a seal
- While maintaining the airways open, give one rescue breath for one second, checking for the chest to rise, then give another rescue breath
- If no signs of life are found, do a quick scan for severe bleeding and CPR if needed (you will learn the skills in chapter 5).

H. A. I. N.E. S. RECOVERY POSITION

The **High Arm Endangered Spine Recovery Position** is used when the person is unconscious and throwing up or when you are alone and must leave the person to get help or equipment. This prevents any vomit from suffocating the injured or ill person.

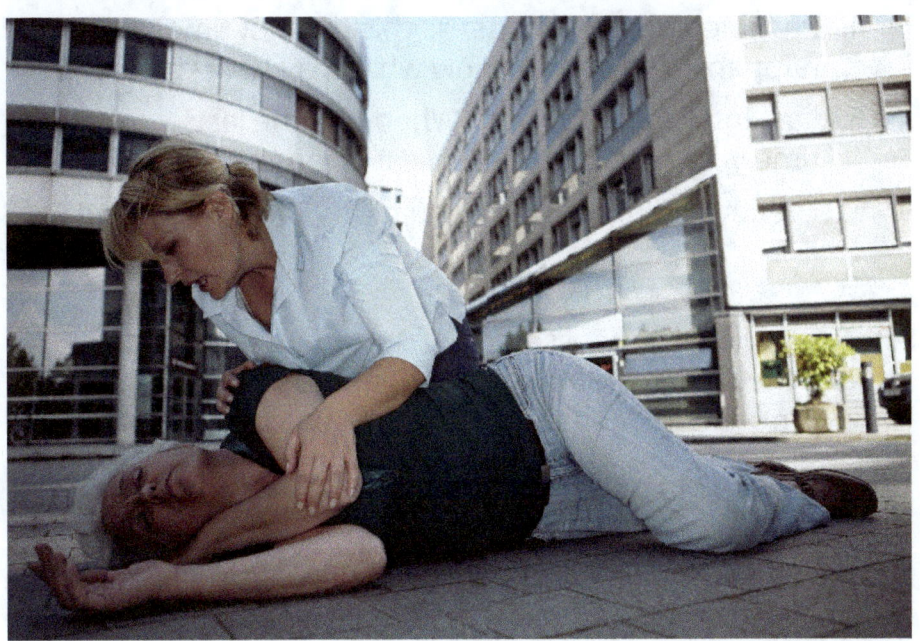

H.A.I.N.E.S. recovery position

CHECKING A CONSCIOUS PERSON

When the ill or injured person is conscious, there are many symptoms and information you don't know. Try to figure out what happened by asking them questions. We use the acronym **SAMPLE** to remember the critical questions for the person's medical assessment.

SAMPLE assessment:

1. Signs and Symptoms: "How are you feeling?"
2. Allergies: "Are you allergic to anything?"
3. Medicine: "Are you taking any medication? What is it for? Do you need it right now? Do you have it with you?"

4. Past Medical Conditions: "Is this the first time this is happening?" "Do you know what may have caused it?"
5. Last Intake and Output: "When was the last time you had something to eat or drink?"
6. Events leading up to the situation: "What happened?"

CHECKING THE PERSON FROM HEAD TO TOE

After conducting your assessment, you need to visually check the person from head to toe to obtain more information about the person's condition.

- Examine the person's head and face
- Check for cuts, bruises, discoloration of the skin, temperature
- Check for a medical tag. This can be a bracelet or necklace with information about their medical history
- Check for any change in their level of alertness and consciousness
- Check for any change in their breathing

CHECKING FOR SHOCK

When the body cannot provide oxygen-rich blood to every part of the body, the injured or ill person will get into shock. This is a life-threatening condition that can lead to death, and you should seek advanced medical care immediately. It is crucial that you recognize the symptoms of shock.

Symptoms of Shock:

- Pale, cool, moist skin
- Rapid breathing
- Excessive Thirst

- Restlessness or irritability
- Vomiting
- Altered level of consciousness

After checking the scene, always use the CHECK, CALL, and CARE steps to determine if there are any life-threatening conditions, including no breathing, trouble breathing, unconsciousness, or severe bleeding. If the person is conscious, the SAMPLE assessment can help determine the care to provide.

CHAPTER

CARDIAC EMERGENCIES

INTRODUCTION

Cardiac emergencies are the number one cause of death in the United States and in many parts of the world. Learning to recognize the signs and symptoms of a cardiac emergency can help maintain life while professional care is on the way. In this chapter, you will learn how to recognize the signs of cardiovascular emergencies, give cardiopulmonary resuscitation (CPR), and use an automated defibrillator (AED).

LEARNING OBJECTIVES

After reading this chapter, you will be able to:

- List the signs and symptoms of a heart attack in males
- List the signs and symptoms of a heart attack in females
- Describe the care needed for someone experiencing a heart attack
- List the signs and symptoms of a stroke
- Demonstrate how to give CPR to an adult, child, and infant

- Demonstrate how to use an AED with an adult, child, and infant

SIGNS OF A HEART ATTACK

A heart attack happens when blood flow to the heart is reduced due to a blockage in an artery. This leads to oxygen deprivation in one part of the heart muscle. The more time passes without adequate oxygen to all parts of the heart, the more serious the damage. Arteries can be blocked due to high cholesterol and fatty deposits.

A heart attack can lead to cardiac arrest when the heart suddenly stops pumping blood to vital organs. Cardiac arrest can be reversed when CPR and defibrillator shocks are administered immediately (or within a few minutes). **Chances of survival drop by 10 percent for every minute defibrillation is delayed.**

SIGNS AND SYMPTOMS OF A HEART ATTACK

The most common symptoms of a heart attack in both men and women include:

- Chest pain that doesn't go away after 3-5 minutes or chest pain that comes and goes. The pain can be described as tightness or pressure in the chest, arm, shoulder, jaw, or stomach
- Problems breathing, shortness of breath, fast breathing
- Pale skin
- Dizziness

- Profuse sweating
- Feeling lightheaded

SIGNS OF A HEART ATTACK IN WOMEN

In addition to the signs of a heart attack listed above, women may also
Experience:

- Pain in the back
- Nausea and vomiting
- Shortness of breath
- Sudden fatigue

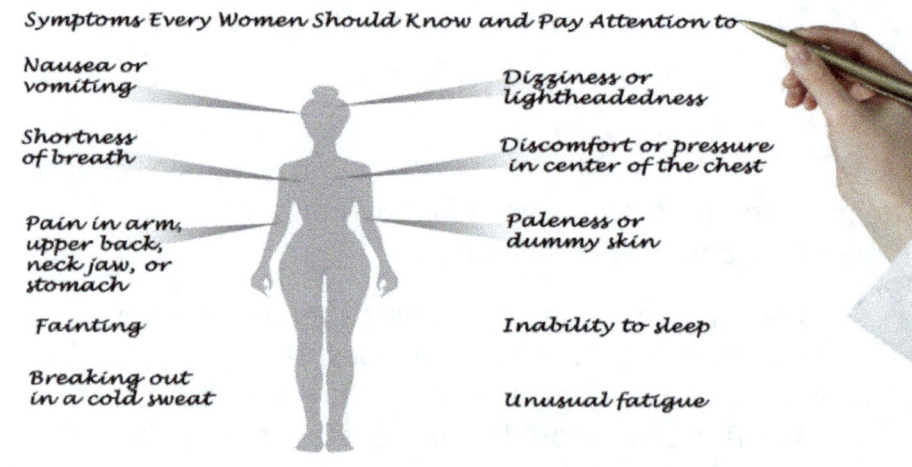

CARE FOR A HEART ATTACK

It is common for people experiencing a heart attack to be in denial. Remember that a heart attack may lead to cardiac arrest and death and that most people who experience a heart attack die within 2 hours of the first symptoms. A person in cardiac arrest will be unconscious and not breathing. Recognizing the signs, calling an ambulance, and caring for the person immediately may prevent further damage to the heart.

- Obtain consent
- Call 911
- Have the person sit and rest comfortably and loosen up tight clothing
- Monitor the person until help arrives
- Ask the person if they have a history of heart disease and if they are on medication for it
- Ask the person if they have known allergies to Aspirin or if their doctor told them they should not take aspirin. If they are not allergic, offer Aspirin at the first signs of a heart attack. Aspirin is a blood thinner that can prevent further artery blockage while waiting for an ambulance. However, do not give aspirin to a person with stomach disease or ulcer or who is taking blood thinners.
- Be prepared to give CPR (**chest compressions** and **rescue breaths**)
- Interview bystanders to obtain more information about the ill person
- Do NOT drive the person to the hospital yourself because you would be unable to help them if the situation worsened.

CPR

CPR stands for **cardiopulmonary resuscitation**. It is a combination of chest compressions and rescue breaths. Giving CPR helps take over the work of the heart and the lungs while waiting for professional care. Understand that CPR only provides a third of the normal blood to the brain. For that reason, in addition to giving CPR, using an AED gives the person a better chance of survival.

Every minute the person is not receiving care reduces the chance of survival by 10%. Knowing what to do and calling 911 right away is critical.

WHEN AND HOW TO GIVE CPR (Adults)

If a conscious person loses consciousness or is already unconscious, follow the steps below to check for responsiveness. Always follow the **CHECK-CALL-CARE:**

- CHECK the scene
- CHECK the person

Checking the Person for Responsiveness:

Use the skills learned for breathing emergencies. Tap the shoulder, and ask:" are you ok?" If there is no response,

- Call 911

If a bystander is available, have them get the AED and first aid kit

- Open the airways to check for breathing by performing the **Head-tilt Chin-lift** technique

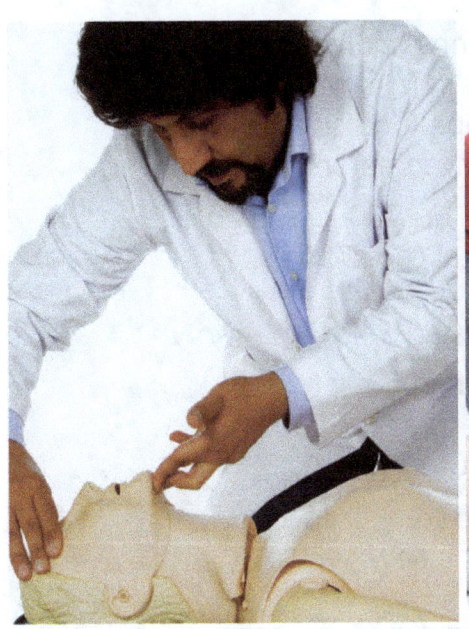 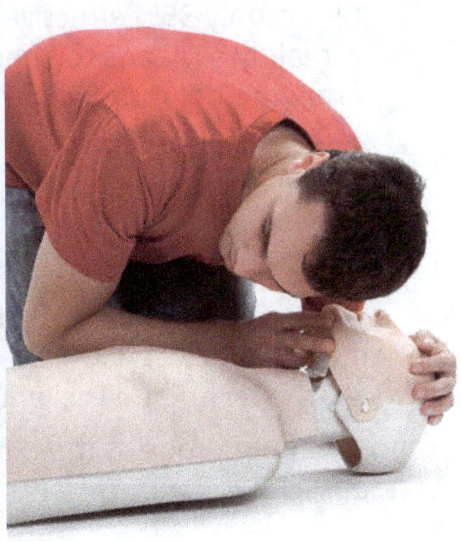

Head-tilt – Chin-lift technique (left)
Look, listen, feel for breathing (right)

- Once the airways are open, look, listen and feel for breathing for no **more than 10 seconds** by placing your ear close to the nose and mouth. In adults and children, maintain the head tilted backward. At the same time, check if you notice the chest rising as a sign of breathing.

- If the person is NOT breathing, ensure they are on a solid surface before giving CPR; providing CPR on a soft surface is ineffective. Give 30 chest compressions followed by two rescue breaths. If you are unable or unwilling to give rescue breaths, give chest compressions continuously.

- CPR is performed in a series of compressions and breaths designed to keep blood circulating until the AED (Automated External Defibrillator) or more advanced medical personnel arrive and take over. CPR is only 35% effective in restarting the heart. It is mainly a means to keep blood circulating long enough until more advanced personnel take over.

- Continue giving CPR until an AED is available or more advanced medical care arrives.

WHEN AND HOW TO GIVE CPR (Child or infant)

When giving CPR to children and infants, follow the same **CHECK-CALL-CARE** steps as for adults; however, the technique is slightly different.

Compare and memorize the differences in care for adults, children, and infants below.

	ADULT	CHILD	INFANT
HAND POSITION	2 Hands in the center of the chest	2 Hands in the center of the chest	2-3 fingers in the center of the chest or 2 thumbs encircling
CHEST COMPRESSION	At least 2 inches deep	About 2 inches deep	About 1.5 inches deep
RESCUE BREATHS	2	2	2
CYCLES	30 chest compressions followed by two breaths	30 chest compressions followed by two breaths	30 chest compressions followed by two breaths
RATE	100 compressions per minute	100 compressions per minute	100 compressions per minute

Continue giving CPR until more advanced care takes over or one of the following situations occurs:

- Scene becomes unsafe
- You are too exhausted to continue
- The person starts breathing on their own
- More advanced medical personnel arrive and assume care

An AED should be used as soon as possible when a person is not breathing. Most AEDs operate the same way. If a bystander is available, have them open the bag and turn the AED while you keep giving CPR. Follow the prompts provided by the AED.

STEPS FOR USING AN AED

- Remove clothing from the chest area
- Place the pads of the AED on the bare chest as shown on the diagram provided with the pads

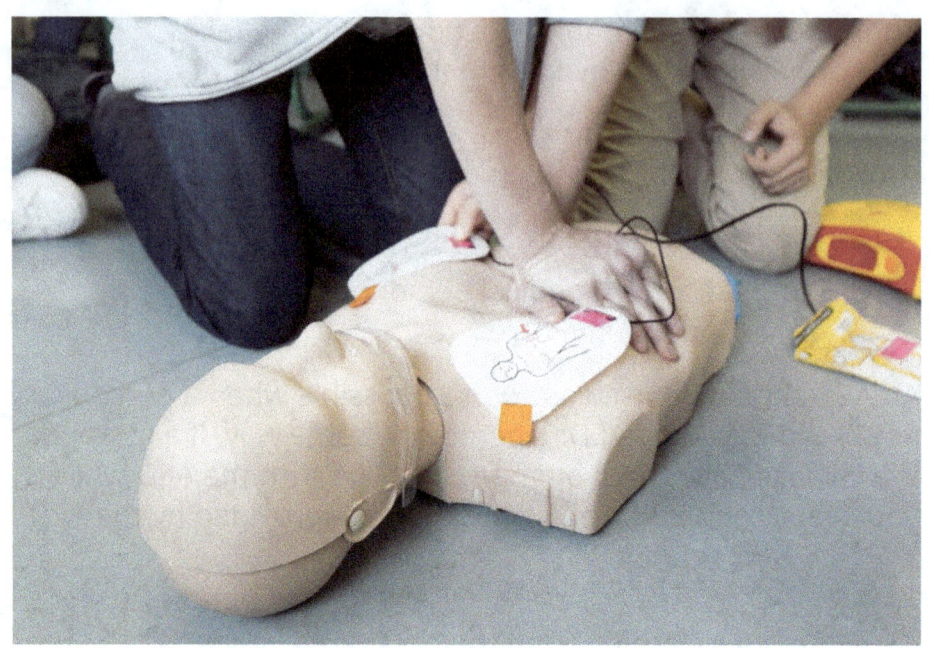

AED pads on the chest

- Plug the connector to the AED, and let the AED analyze the heart rhythm. The AED will guide you through the entire process, letting you know if or when to start giving CPR. If shock is necessary, the AED will prompt you to give a shock. No one should be touching the person when the shock is administered
- Loudly and clearly shout:" Everybody stands clear!" before a shock is administered
- Deliver the shock by pressing the shock button on the AED

SKILLS REVIEW

GIVING CPR TO AN ADULT OR CHILD

- Check the scene and check for responsiveness. If the person is not responding and not breathing, call 911 and begin CPR
- Give 30 chest compressions at least two inches deep in adults and about 2 inches deep in children
    - Place one hand on top of the other in the center of the chest

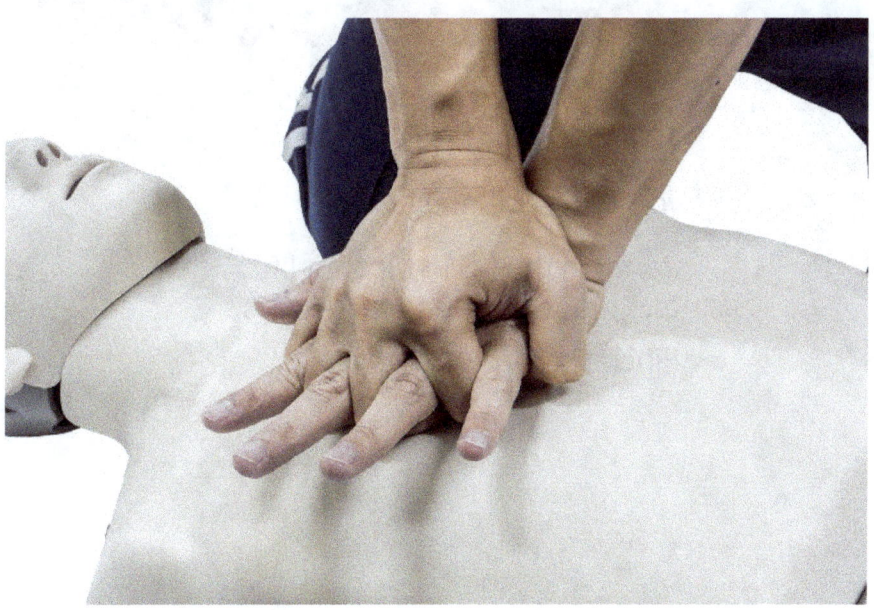

    - Stand on your knees with your shoulders stacked directly above your hands

Cardiac Emergencies

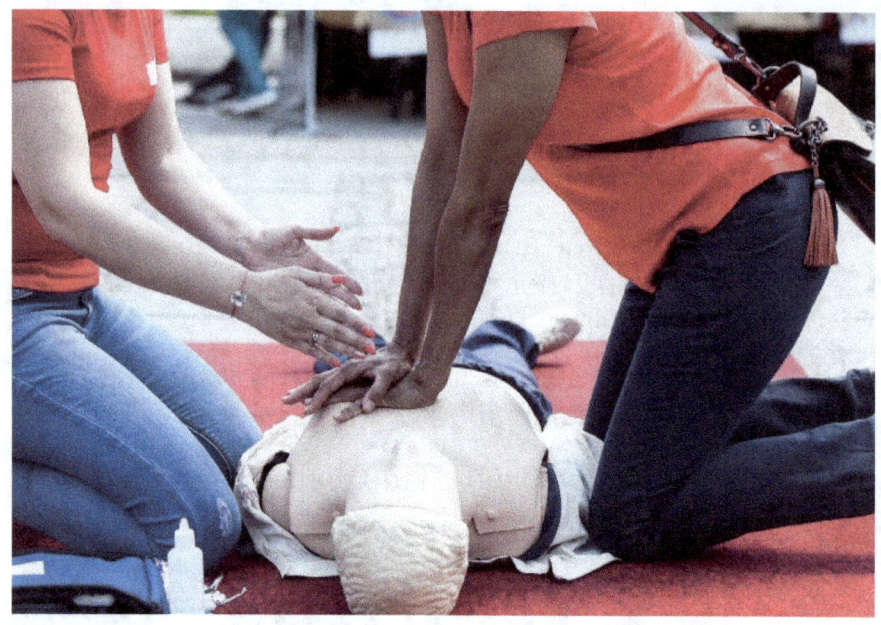

- Give 30 chest compressions at a rate of 100-120 compressions per minute
- Give two rescue breaths:
  - Perform the head-tilt chin-lift technique to open the airways,
  - Pinch the person's nose.

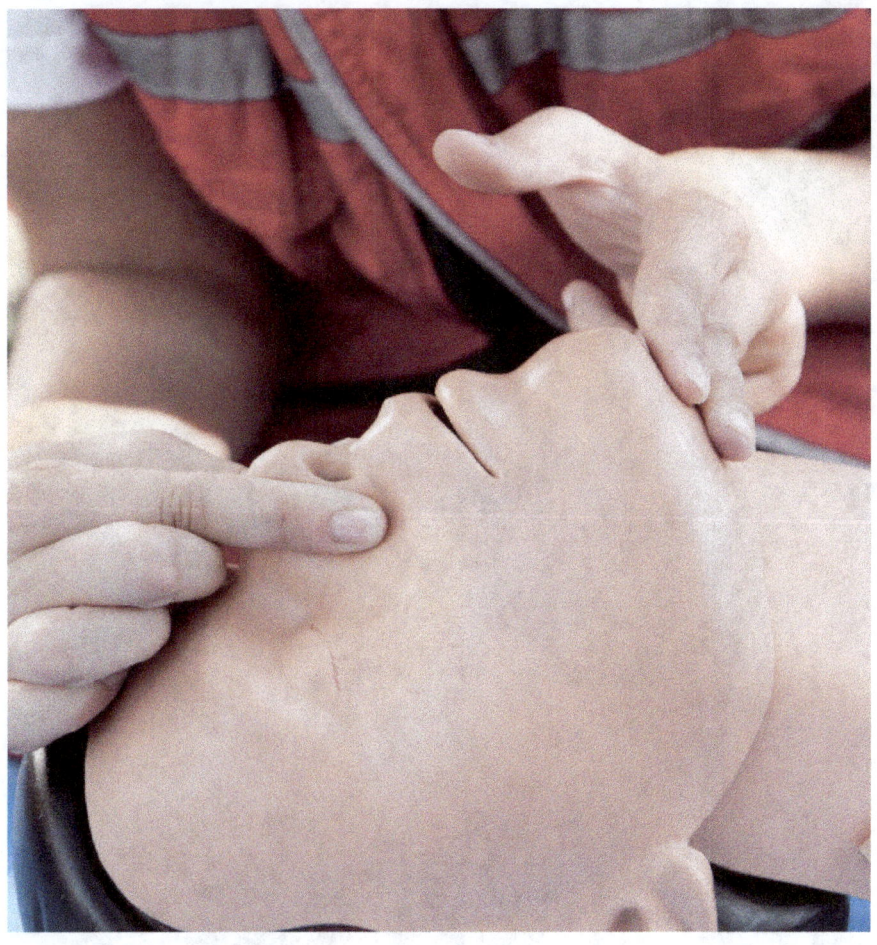

- o   Place a breathing barrier over the person's mouth
- o   Seal your mouth around the person's mouth and blow for about one second, checking that the chest rises. If the chest does not rise, re-tilt the head back. If the breath still doesn't get through, an object might be blocking the airways.

Rescue breath

Continue giving sets of 30 chest compressions and two rescue breaths until

- The person starts breathing again
- Someone qualified or better qualified than you takes over
- The scene becomes unsafe
- You are too exhausted to continue
- The scene becomes unsafe
- An AED is available to use

To watch the video tutorial, point your phone's camera to the QR code below and tap the icon on your screen to access the video link.

Adult CPR Tutorial

GIVING CPR TO AN INFANT

- Check for responsiveness by flicking the bottom of the infant's foot, and shouting their name if you know it

- If the infant does not react, check for breathing by placing one ear close to the infant's airways and checking for their chest to rise. Do not tilt the head back because their necks are very fragile
- If there is no signs of breathing, place the infant on a firm surface and begin CPR

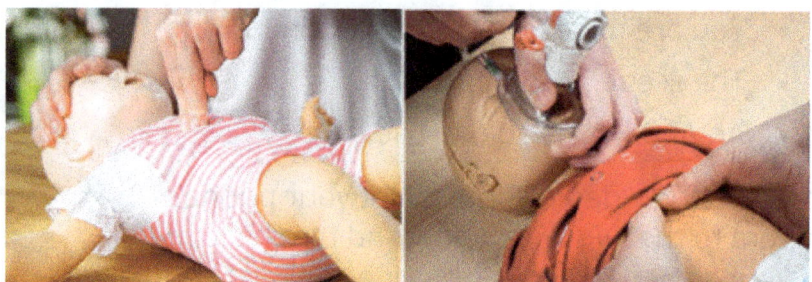

Two fingers method / Two thumbs encircling method

- Give 30 chest compressions:
    o Place one hand on the infant's forehead
    o Use two or three fingers to give chest compressions 1½ inches deep in the center of the chest, just below the nipple line. Alternatively, you can use the two thumbs encircling method for chest compressions by placing two thumbs in the center of the chest and using the rest of the fingers to wrap the infant's ribs
    o Give 100-120 compressions per minute
- Give two rescue breaths. First, use a breathing barrier to cover the infant's mouth and nose.

- Make a seal with your mouth over the infant's mouth and nose
- Blow into their mouth for about one second, checking that their chest rises
- Repeat with a second rescue breath

If the first rescue breath does not cause the infant's chest to rise, ensure a proper seal before giving the second rescue breath. If the second rescue breath does not make the infant's chest rise, an object may be blocking their airways. After the next set of chest compressions and before attempting additional rescue breaths, open the infant's mouth, look for any objects and, if seen, remove it using a finger sweep. Continue to check the infant's mouth for objects after each set of compressions until the rescue breaths go in.

Continue giving sets of 30 chest compressions and two rescue breaths until

- The infant starts breathing again
- Someone qualified or better qualified takes over
- The scene becomes unsafe
- You are too exhausted to continue
- An AED is available

To watch the video tutorial, point your phone's camera to the QR code below and tap the icon on your screen to access the video link.

Infant CPR Tutorial

SCAN ME

USING AN AED

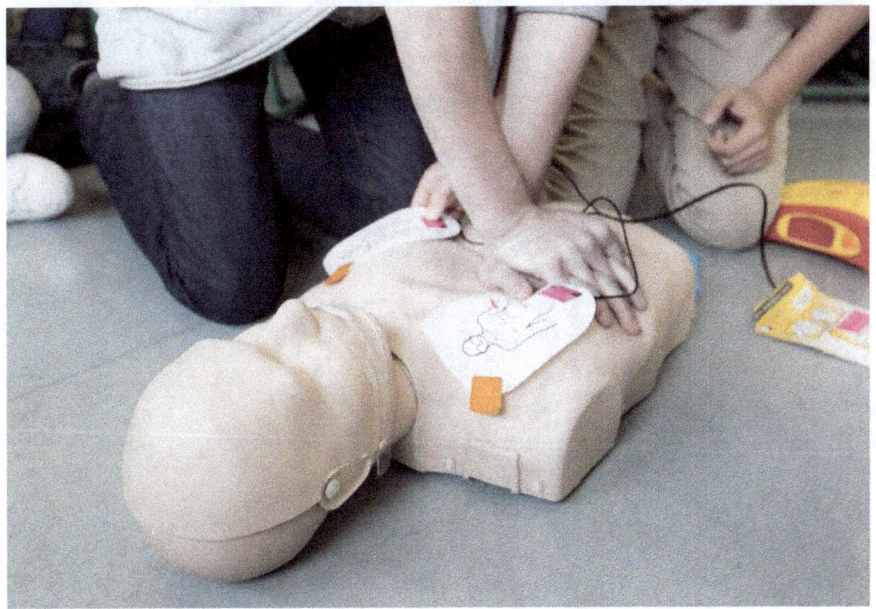

Mannequin with AED pads on the chest

Use an AED as soon as possible. If a bystander is present, continue giving CPR, and direct the bystander to open the AED:

- Place the pads on the chest as shown on the AED's images. With infants, place one pad in the center of their chest and the other one in the center of their back
- Plug in the connector on the AED
- Turn on the AED

Follow the prompt given by the AED. If the AED directs you to "stand clear", ensure no one is touching the person. Continue giving CPR if the AED prompts you to do so.

To watch the video tutorial, point your phone's camera to the QR code below and tap the icon on your screen to access the video link.

Adult CPR with AED

CHAPTER

BREATHING EMERGENCIES

INTRODUCTION

A breathing emergency occurs when a respiratory problem becomes life-threatening. It happens when oxygen is unable to reach the lungs properly.

This chapter will teach you how to identify the causes and signs of breathing and asthma emergencies. You will also learn how to give care to someone experiencing a breathing emergency.

LEARNING OBJECTIVES

After reading this chapter, you will be able to:

- Recognize a breathing emergency
- Recognize the symptoms of asthma
- Demonstrate how to provide care for a conscious adult, child, or infant who is choking
- Demonstrate how to provide care for an unconscious adult, child, or infant who is choking

- Demonstrate care for someone experiencing an asthma attack

The most common Respiratory Distress occurs when oxygen cannot reach the lungs freely, and breathing becomes compromised. Respiratory distress can lead to Respiratory Arrest, meaning there is no more breathing. There are two types of breathing emergencies:

Anatomical Airway Obstruction is due to the swollen tissues of the tongue and throat that block part or all air from reaching the lungs.

Mechanical Airway Obstruction refers to any object, food, or fluid, including vomit and blood or asthma that prevents air from moving freely to the lungs.

CAUSES OF RESPIRATORY DISTRESS AND RESPIRATORY ARREST

- Choking
- Drowning
- Heart attack
- Illness
- Asthma or other respiratory conditions
- Emotional distress
- Congestive heart failure
- Allergic reaction
- Poisoning
- Drug
- Injury to the head, chest, lungs, or abdomen

SIGNS OF RESPIRATORY DISTRESS AND ARREST IN ADULTS

- Trouble breathing
- Shallow breathing
- Slow or fast breathing
- Gasping for air
- Chest pain
- Making unusual sounds
- Flushed, ashen, or pale skin
- Dizziness

SIGNS OF RESPIRATORY DISTRESS IN CHILDREN

- Increased heart rate
- Fast or slow breathing
- Agitation
- Fast heart rate
- Noisy breathing
- Flaring nostrils
- Drowsiness

SIGNS OF RESPIRATORY ARREST IN CHILDREN

- Absence of breathing
- Non-responsive

- Ashen skin color

CARE FOR RESPIRATORY DISTRESS AND RESPIRATORY ARREST

Follow the **CHECK-CALL-CARE** you learned in the previous chapter for any type of emergency.

- Check the scene to ensure it is safe for you to proceed
- Check the person for life-threatening conditions. Recall that life-threatening conditions include problems breathing, no breathing, unconsciousness, and severe bleeding
- If the person is conscious, obtain consent and
    - o proceed with the SAMPLE interview assessment
    - o Continue to give care, reassure the person, and monitor the situation
    - o A conscious person can become unconscious at any time, so be prepared to provide care to an unconscious person
- If the person has a life-threatening condition, call 911, and then
    - o begin CPR if they are unconscious and not breathing
    - o Use an AED as soon as one is available

USING THE SAMPLE INTERVIEW ASSESSMENT

The SAMPLE interview is used to gather critical information about the nature of the person's illness or injury.

- S = Signs and symptoms. Use your senses to observe unusual symptoms. Visually check the person from head to toe. Ask the person to describe their feelings. Check if they're wearing a medical bracelet.
- A = Allergies. Ask the person if they have any known allergies or if they have their medication with them.
- M = Medications. Ask the person if they take either prescribed or over-the-counter medication, the name of the medication, and when they last took it.
- P = Pertinent medical history. Ask the person whether they have any medical conditions.
- L = Last food or drink. Ask the person when they last had something to eat or drink, what they ate or drank, and how much.
- E = Events leading up to the incident. Ask the person what was happening and what they were doing just before they began to feel ill or were injured.

ASTHMA

Asthma is a condition in which the airways and lungs get inflamed and block normal air passage to the lungs, making breathing difficult. In addition, certain conditions or substances can trigger asthma attacks.

Asthma Triggers
- Fear and anxiety
- Dust
- Smoke
- Certain animals

- Weather conditions
- Pollution
- Perfume
- Exercise
- Medication
- Respiratory infection

When triggers are present, a person can go into an asthma attack.

SIGNS OF AN ASTHMA ATTACK

- Wheezing sound when breathing
- Problem breathing
- Shortness of breath
- Sweating
- Tightness in the chest
- Feeling fear
- Confusion

Care for an Asthma Attack

- Reassure the person
- Ask them if they have any asthma medication. If so, help the person take their medication
- Have them sit comfortably and loosen up any tight clothing around the neck and chest areas
- If the condition does not improve, call 911

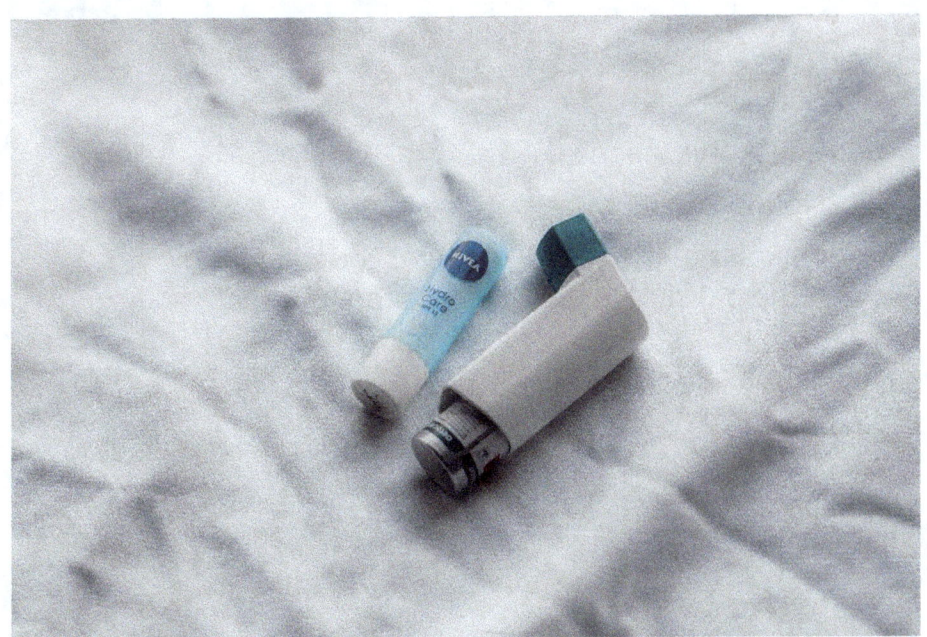

CHOKING

Choking happens when the airways are partially or entirely blocked by an object, food, vomit, fluid, or swelling of the throat or mouth. When the airways are partially blocked, air can still go through the lungs, and the person may still be able to breathe with difficulties. They will cough to try to dislodge the object. Partial airway obstruction can turn into a complete blockage.

If the airways are completely blocked, the person cannot speak, cough, cry or breathe and will soon collapse and become unconscious. In addition, the person's face may turn a bluish color. In this situation, call 911 before giving care.

CARE FOR CONSCIOUS CHOKING – Adults and Child

- Check the scene
- Obtain consent
- Encourage the person to keep coughing to help dislodge the object or food

Universal signal for choking

- Ask the person if they want you to call 911
- Stand next to the person with one foot in front of the person and one foot behind the person
- Slide your arm under the person's armpit and across the chest for support

- Using the heel of your hand, proceed with five back blows behind the shoulder blades. The back blows are designed to help dislodge the object blocking the airways

Back blows

- If the person is still choking after five back blows, proceed with five abdominal thrusts. First, make a fist and wrap it with the palm of your other hand. Stand behind the person, and place your fist above the person's navel. With a child, get on your knees behind the child. The abdominal thrusts create pressure that helps force the blocked object out of the airways.

Abdominal Thrust

- Continue alternating with five back blows and five abdominal thrusts until the person stops choking, the food or object blocking the airways is expelled, or the person loses consciousness.

If You Are Alone

If you are choking and are alone, you can give yourself abdominal thrusts using your fist. The other option is to lean over the back of a chair or a railing to try dislodging the object.

If the Person Is Pregnant

If the person is pregnant, give the person chest thrusts instead of abdominal thrusts.

CARE FOR CONSCIOUS CHOKING – Infants

When an infant is conscious but unable to breathe, place the infant on your forearm and perform five back blows and five abdominal thrusts using two fingers.

- First, place the infant on your forearm face-up. Then, ensure that the infant's head is supported at all times by cradling the back of their head in your hand.
- Holding the front of the infant's head and their jaw with your thumb and fingers, flip them over so that the infant is now facing down and resting on your other forearm.

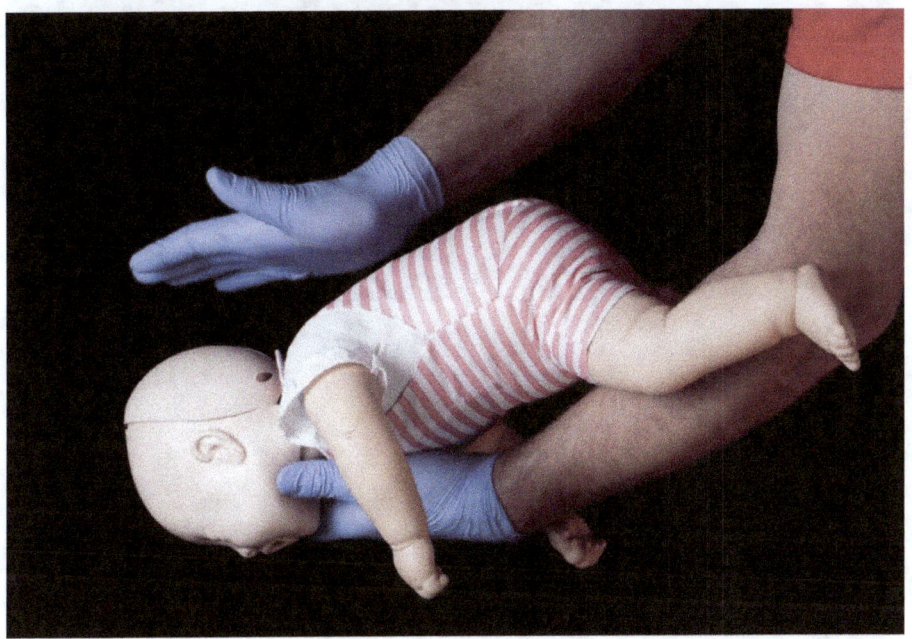

Back blows in infants

- Bend over, and rest your forearm holding the infant on your thigh so that their head is lower than their hips.

Breathing Emergencies 69

- Continue giving five back blows and five abdominal thrusts using 2-3 fingers until the infant is able to breathe or cry normally or becomes unconscious.

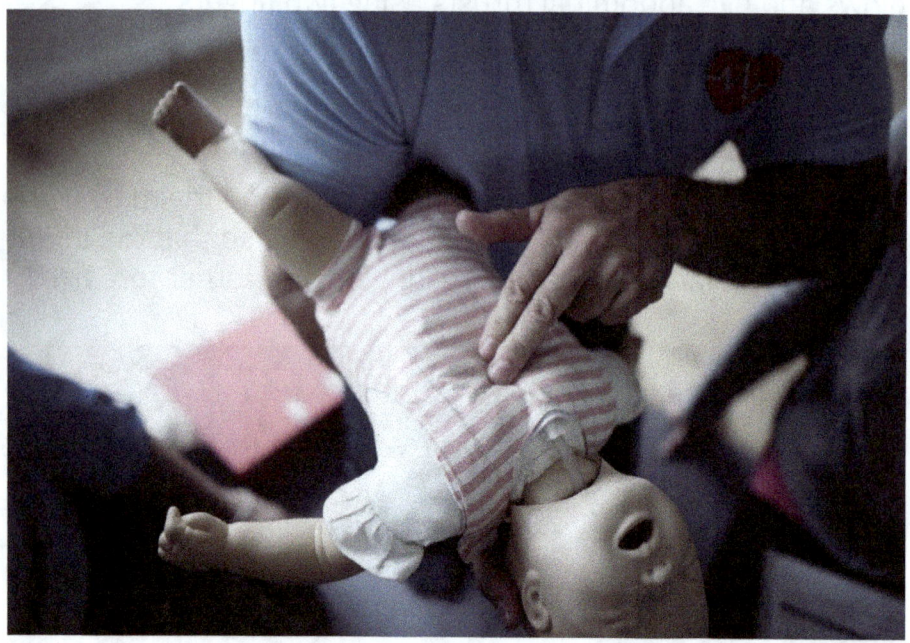

Abdominal thrust on infant

CARE FOR UNCONSCIOUS CHOKING- Adult and Child

Giving five back blows and five abdominal thrusts may not always work, and the person may become unconscious. When this happens:

- Lower the person to the floor
- Call 911 if it hasn't been done yet

- Open the person's mouth to check if you can see the object or food blocking the airways. If you see something, wear gloves and use one finger to scoop the object out of the mouth
- Open the airways using the **head-tilt chin-lift** method learned in the previous chapters and give two rescue breaths. As you give two breaths, check if their chest rises with each rescue breath. If their chest is not rising, give **modified CPR**.

Modified CPR

Modified CPR is used for an unconscious choking adult, and child. Modified CPR is similar to standard CPR, but you check for the foreign object blocking the airways between the 30 chest compressions and the two rescue breaths. Continue giving modified CPR until:

- the object is removed, and the chest rises with each rescue breath
- the person starts breathing on their own
- someone with the same or higher training than you takes over
- you are too exhausted to continue
- the scene becomes unsafe

CARE FOR UNCONSCIOUS CHOKING - Infant

A conscious choking infant can become unconscious at any time. When providing care to an unconscious choking infant, perform modified CPR using the CPR technique you learned for infants:

- Give 30 chest compressions about 1 ½ inches deep
- Check for foreign objects or food in the mouth. If you find an object, remove it using your little finger to swipe it out
- Give two rescue breaths
- Continue giving modified CPR until:
- The object is removed, and the chest rises with each rescue breath
- the infant starts breathing on their own
- someone with the same or higher training takes over
- you are too tired to continue
- the scene becomes unsafe

After giving care to a choking person, they should be evaluated by a medical doctor to rule out any potential injury to the airways.

PREVENTING BREATHING EMERGENCIES IN CHILDREN AND INFANTS

Choking is very common in young children because they put everything in their mouths. Children should be supervised when eating and playing. Make sure children remain seated when they eat. You should not give the following food to children:

- Popcorn

- Grapes
- Chewing gum
- Hard or gooey candy

When giving toys to children, ensure they are age appropriate by reading the fine print on the back of the toys' packages. Supervise young children at all times when playing with toys.

Be especially careful with the following objects:

- Marbles
- Buttons
- Coins
- Batteries
- Safety pins

Child playing with toys

SKILLS REVIEW

CARING FOR AN ADULT WHO IS CHOKING

If the person is able to speak to you or is coughing forcefully, obtain consent

- Encourage the person to keep coughing and be prepared to provide CPR if the person collapses and becomes unconscious.
- If the person cannot speak to you or is coughing weakly, call 911 and obtain an AED whenever available.
- Give five back blows:
    - Position yourself to the side and slightly behind the person. Place one arm diagonally across the person's chest (to provide support) and bend the person forward at the waist so that the person's upper body is as close to parallel to the ground as possible.
    - Firmly strike the person between the shoulder blades with the palm of your hand.

- Next, position yourself behind the person, and give five abdominal thrusts:
    - Have the person stand up straight. Stand behind the person with one foot in front of the other for balance, and wrap your arms around the person's waist.
    - Ask the person to point to their navel.
    - Make a fist with one hand, keeping your thumb against the person above their navel.
    - Use your other hand to cover your fist.
    - Give five abdominal thrusts pulling firmly inwards and upward.

Continue giving sets of five back blows and five abdominal thrusts until:

- The person can cough forcefully, speak, cry or breathe.
- The person becomes unresponsive.

If the person becomes unresponsive, gently lower him or her to the floor and begin modified CPR, starting with chest compressions. After each set of compressions and before attempting rescue breaths, open the person's mouth, look for the object and remove it if seen. Never put your finger in the person's mouth unless you see the object.

CARING FOR AN INFANT WHO IS CHOKING

- If a caregiver is present, obtain consent and ask them to call 911
- Cradle the infant's face and position it down on your forearm. Sit down and rest your forearm on your thigh for support, making sure the hips are higher than their shoulders. This will help dislodge the object or food blocking the airways. Support the infant's jaw with your fingers. Give five back blows with the palm of your hand

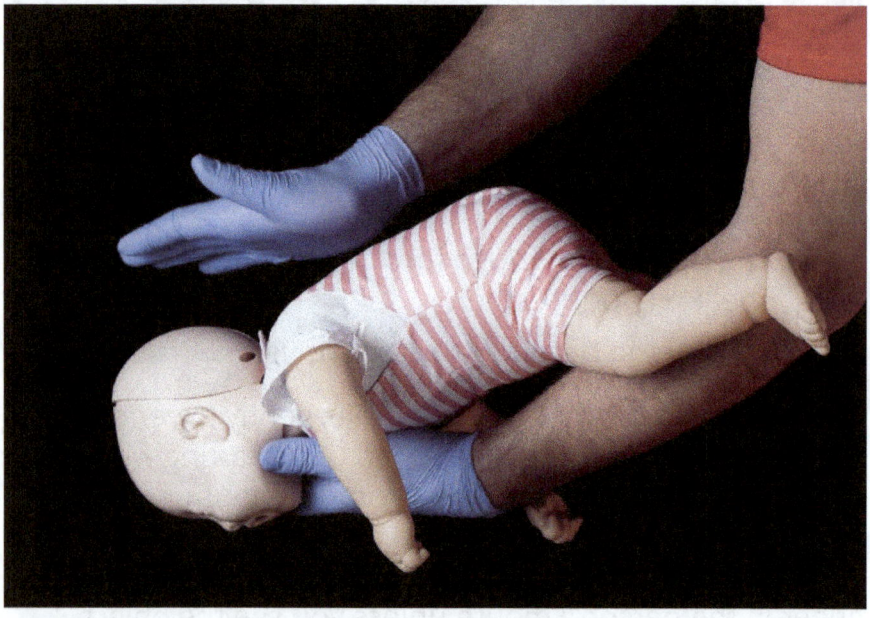

- Turn the infant over onto your other arm so that he or she is facing up. Use your supporting hand to support the infant's head

- Using two fingers in the center of the chest, give five abdominal chest compressions 1½ inches deep

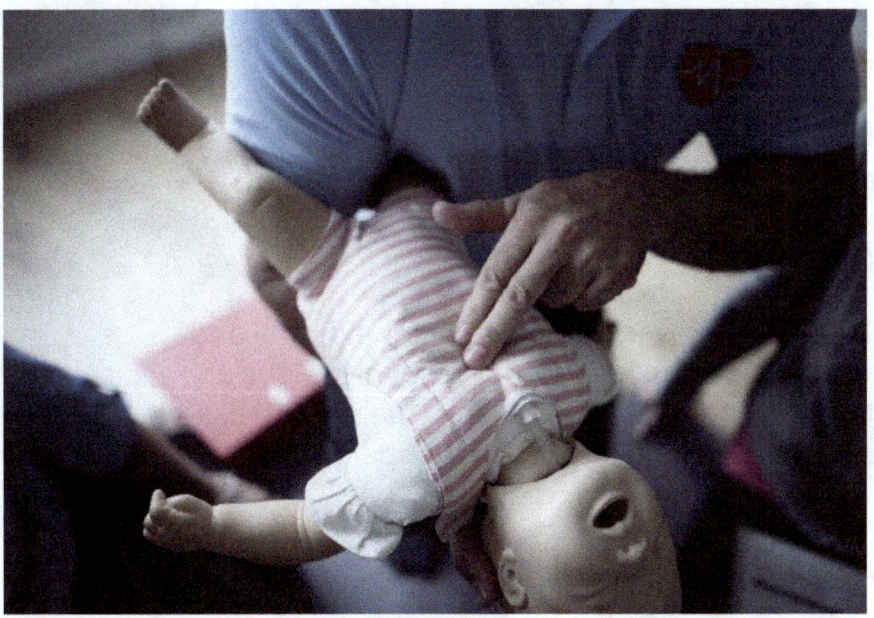

Continue giving five back blows and five chest compressions until the infant starts breathing normally again or loses consciousness. If the infant loses consciousness, obtain an AED, if possible, and begin modified CPR.

CHAPTER 7

BLEEDING AND SHOCK

INTRODUCTION

This chapter covers how to care for external and internal bleeding and how to recognize signs of shock. In addition, you will learn the skills to use a tourniquet and how to care for impaled objects.

LEARNING OBJECTIVES

- After reading this chapter, you will be able to:
- Differentiate between arterial, venous, and capillary bleeding
- Identify the signs of life-threatening external bleeding
- Describe the signs of life-threatening internal bleeding
- Demonstrate how to care for external bleeding
- Explain how to care for minor internal bleeding
- Demonstrate the proper technique for using a tourniquet

BLOOD AND BLOOD VESSELS

The main functions of the blood include:

- Transporting oxygen-rich blood and nutrients to the organs and lungs
- Removing waste to be filtered by the liver and kidneys
- Forming clots to stop excess blood loss
- Maintaining body temperature
- Carrying antibodies to protect against diseases

Think of blood vessels as channels transporting blood throughout the body. For example, **arteries** carry blood away from the heart. **Veins** carry blood back to the heart and transport waste products to the kidneys and lungs for elimination. **Capillaries** connect arteries to veins and exchange oxygen and carbon dioxide. They are microscopic blood vessels that move oxygen from the blood into the cells and waste products from the cells to small veins.

Arterial blood is under a lot of pressure and can result in severe life-threatening blood loss in case of an injury. This makes it more challenging to control. In addition, arterial bleeding can shoot or spur rapidly out of a wound, making it difficult to manage.

Venous bleeding is less severe than arterial bleeding but can still be life-threatening. For that reason, it still requires immediate attention.

Capillary bleeding is the most common type of bleeding you will encounter. It is less severe and easier to control than other types of bleeding because capillary blood is under less pressure, tends to be minor, and clots quickly.

CARE FOR MINOR EXTERNAL BLEEDING

In case of minor external bleeding, apply direct pressure to the wound. This restricts blood flow to the injury and facilitates clotting.

- Wear disposable gloves
- Use a sterile dressing directly on the wound
- Have the person apply direct pressure to the dressing for a few minutes
- Wash the wound with water and soap
- Cover the wound with a dressing and a bandage
- Remove and dispose of the gloves
- Wash your hands thoroughly with warm water and soap

CARE FOR SEVERE EXTERNAL BLEEDING

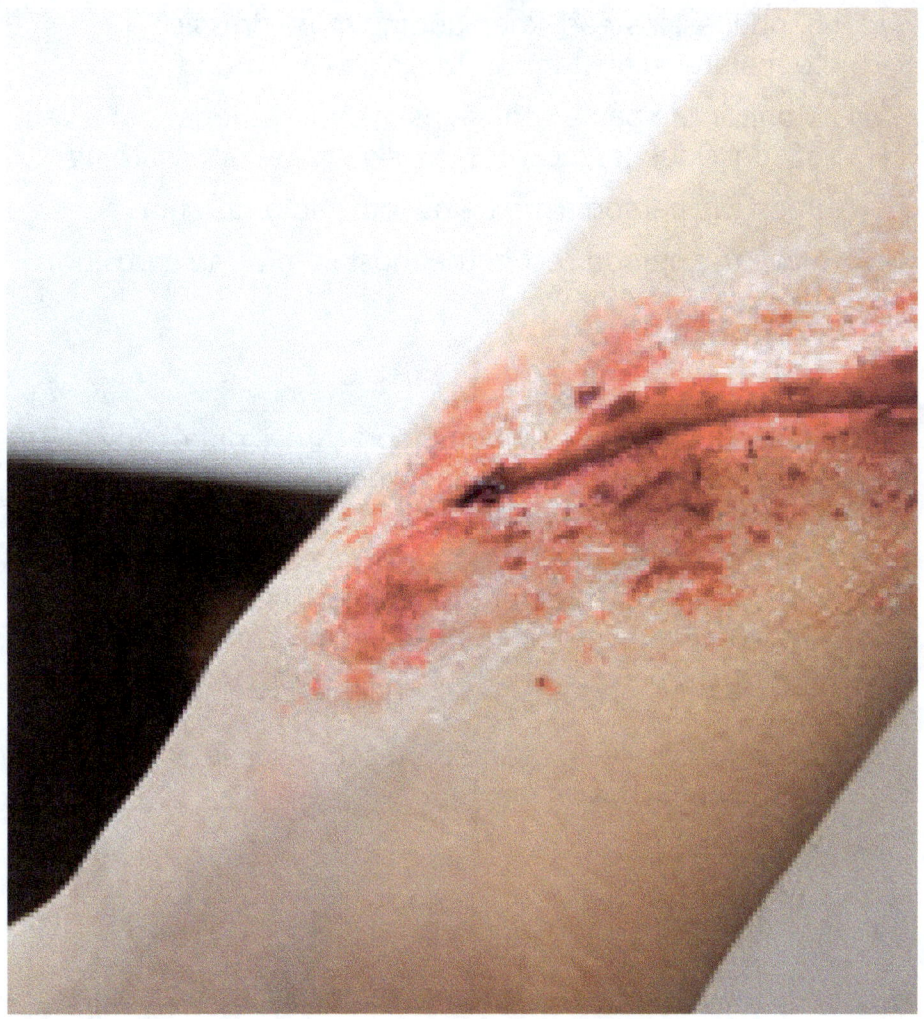

Call 911 if bleeding is severe and provide first aid:

- Wear disposable gloves
- Use a sterile dressing directly on the wound
- Apply a pressure bandage over the sterile dressing

- Add more dressing if it becomes soaked with blood. DO NOT remove the blood-soaked bandages; instead, keep adding more dressing to maintain constant pressure on the wound
- Monitor the person for signs of shock, changes in levels of consciousness, confusion, skin color, or breathing
- Keep the person from being too cold or too hot
- Have the person rest in the most comfortable position

CARE FOR INTERNAL BLEEDING

Internal bleeding happens when blood comes out of any of the blood vessels but remains underneath the skin. It can be something as minor as a bruise or something life-threatening, such as blunt trauma to an organ. However, there is often no or little external sign of internal injury. Therefore, this type of bleeding may not be noticeable immediately.

Look for the following signs of internal bleeding:

- The injured area may look bruised, swollen, pale, or bluish, and feel tender
- Distended abdomen
- The skin may feel cool or moist
- The injured extremity may be bluish or pale
- The person may vomit blood or feel excessively thirsty
- Rapid breathing
- Altered levels of consciousness or loss of consciousness
- Bleeding from any orifice

In case of severe internal bleeding, call 911 right away. This is a very serious situation that requires immediate medical care. There is not much you can do to stop internal bleeding; however, you can provide general care until the ambulance arrives:

- Reassure the person
- Have the person rest in the most comfortable position
- Keep the person from becoming too cold or too hot
- Monitor breathing
- Monitor levels of consciousness

USING A MANUFACTURED TOURNIQUET

A tourniquet is a tight band applied to the extremities to limit severe blood loss. Tourniquets are used as a last resort when other attempts to control bleeding have failed. Once secured, the tourniquet should not be removed until medical care arrives.

- Place the tourniquet about two inches above the injury but not directly on a joint
- Thread the tag end of the strap through the buckle
- Pull the strap tight
- Twist the rod until the bleeding stops
- Record the time the tourniquet was applied

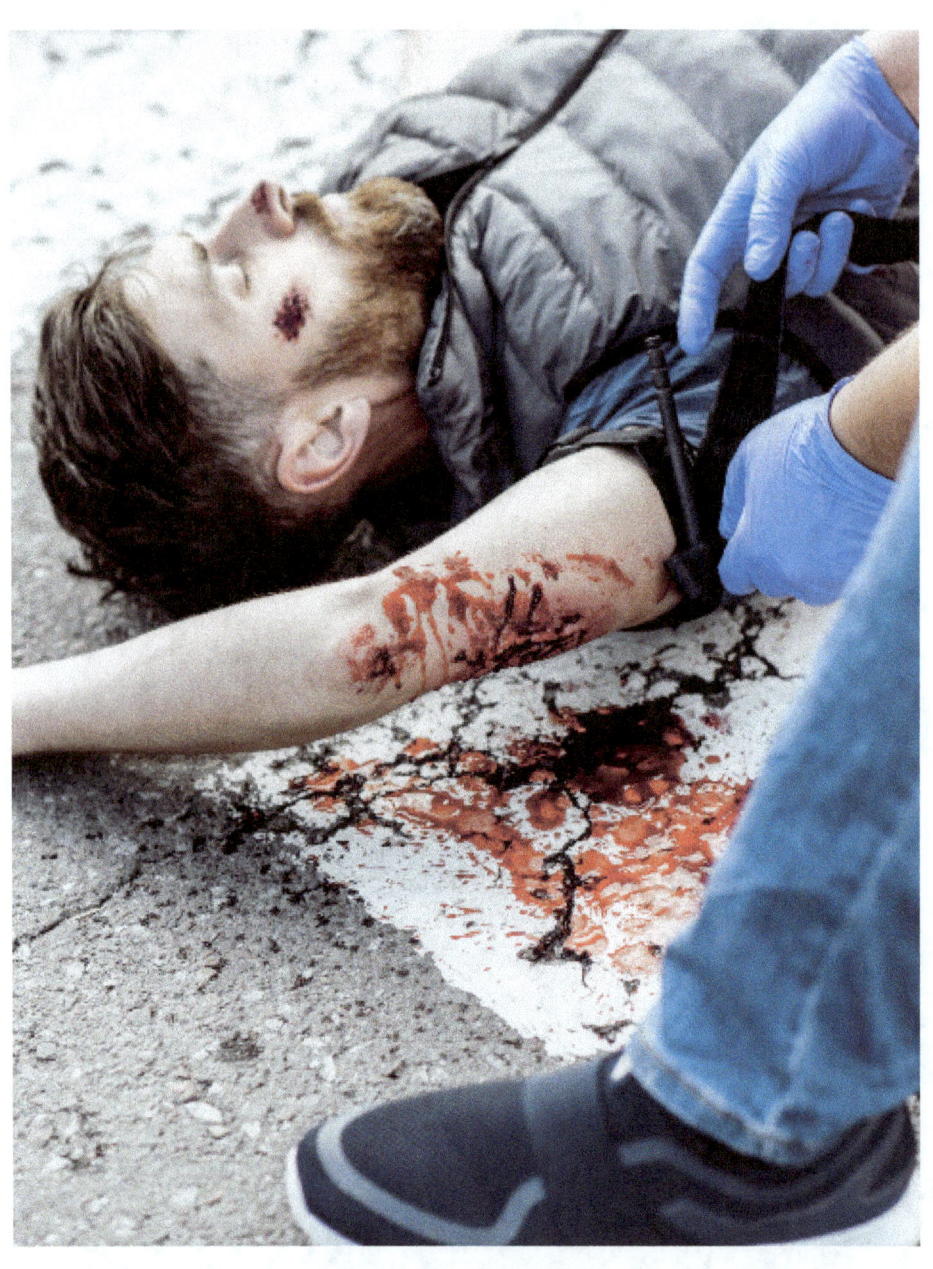

IMPALED OBJECT

When dealing with an impaled object, the object should be left in place. Attempting to remove the object can cause more damage, more pain, and more bleeding. Instead, leave the object in the position in which it is found. Try to stabilize the object with rolled bandages:

- Call 911
- Control bleeding around the object
- Secure the object with rolled bandages
- Monitor the person

Exception: an impaled object may need to be removed if its location can block the airways or if it prevents or interferes with giving CPR.

SHOCK

When oxygenated blood is unable to reach all vital organs such as the lungs, heart, and brain, the person can go into shock. This can occur due to severe bleeding, failure of the heart functions to pump blood throughout the body, or injury to the blood vessels.

SIGNS OF SHOCK

- Pale bluish skin
- Altered levels of consciousness
- Excessive thirst
- Fast heart rate
- Nausea or vomiting

CARE FOR SHOCK

- Follow the CHECK-CALL-CARE steps
- Call 911
- Reassure the person
- Have the person rest in the most comfortable position
- Keep the person from getting too cold or hot
- Monitor the person
- Do not give the person anything to drink or eat as they may require surgery

Be aware that young children may go into shock if they have severe diarrhea or vomiting for long periods of time. Bring the child or infant to a local hospital if you are unable to replace lost fluids or if there has been excessive vomiting or diarrhea.

SKILLS REVIEW

CONTROLLING EXTERNAL BLEEDING

- Wash your hands and wear gloves and protective eyewear
- Cover the wound with a sterile gauze or clean cloth
- Apply direct pressure
- Maintain pressure until bleeding stops. If the gauze becomes saturated with blood, add additional gauze. Do not remove the pressure
- Use a roller bandage to keep the gauze in place

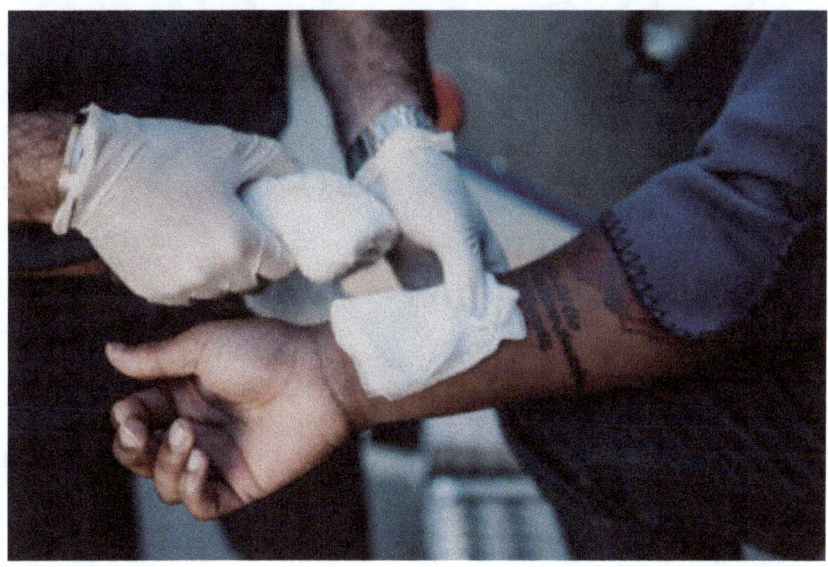

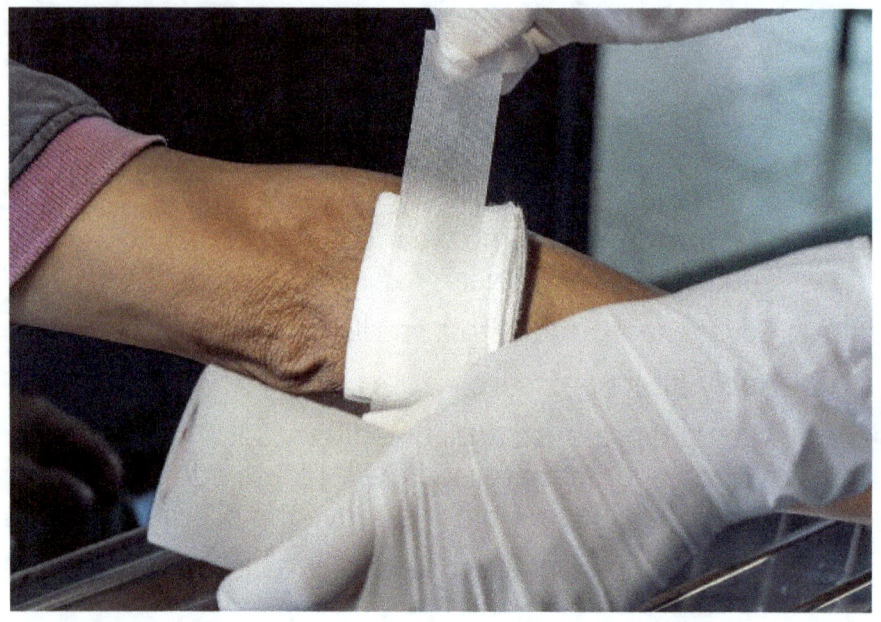

- Remove your gloves and wash your hands.

Protect yourself with protective gloves and goggles when caring for external bleeding. If possible, ask the injured person to apply pressure to their wounds.

CHAPTER 8

SOFT TISSUE INJURIES
Open and Closed Wounds, Burns

INTRODUCTION

The soft tissues include the skin, muscles, and fat. In this chapter, we will discuss the different types of injuries to the soft tissues, such as scrapes, bruises, and burns. You will also learn how to recognize open and closed wounds and care for more severe injuries to the soft tissues that can be life-threatening, such as lacerations and stab wounds.

This chapter allows you to review some of the skills learned in the previous chapter on bleeding.

LEARNING OBJECTIVES

After reading this chapter, you will be able to:

- Explain the difference between closed and open wounds
- Demonstrate how to care for closed wounds
- Demonstrate how to care for open wounds

- Describe how to care for thermal, chemical, electrical, and radiation burns
- Describe the steps to take during lightning

WOUNDS are injuries to the soft tissues. They can be **open** with a break in the skin or **closed**, with the skin intact but bleeding underneath.

OPEN WOUNDS

Open wounds can be as minor as a scrape on the skin's surface and as severe as an amputation. First, let's look at the different types of open wounds.

Abrasions

Abrasions occur when the surface of the skin has been scraped away. There is no or little bleeding with abrasions; however, bacteria can be present and pass through the skin.

Lacerations

Lacerations occur when the skin has been broken, typically by a sharp object such as broken glass or a knife. Bleeding can be heavy, and infections are expected if the laceration is not cleaned.

Avulsions

- An avulsion is an injury in which a piece of skin and the underneath tissues have been entirely or partially torn away, leaving the skin hanging loosely. Bleeding can be significant depending on how much tissue is involved.

Amputations

Amputations refer to an injury in which an extremity, such as a finger, has been severed completely. Reattachment of the body part can sometimes be possible.

CARE FOR AMPUTATION

- Call 911
- Put on disposable gloves
- Apply pressure directly to the wound using a clean dressing until the bleeding stops
- Apply a bandage over the dressing to maintain pressure on the wound
- Add more bandages if blood soaks through. Never remove the soaked bandages
- Look for the severed body part or have a bystander look for the severed body part while you are caring for the open wound
- Wrap the severed body part in sterile gauze or a clean cloth that is kept moist with saline solution
- Place the body part in a plastic bag or container. The bag should be sealed and have the injured person's name and the time of the amputation on it
- Place the plastic bag or container in a larger bag or another container filled with ice and water. Do not place the severed body part directly in contact with ice
- Ensure the bag or container goes to the hospital with the injured person
- Have the person rest in the most comfortable position

PENETRATION AND EMBEDDED OBJECT

When a sharp object pierces the skin and sometimes goes through the tissues underneath, it is called penetration. When the object remains in the wound, it is called an **embedded object.** These types of injuries are at high risk of infection.

In the case of an embedded object:

- Call 911
- Have the person lay down
- Stabilize the object by gently placing gauze around it
- Place roller bandages around the object

In case of an **embedded object in the eye,** do not attempt to remove the object. Instead:

- Call 911
- Have the person lay down
- Stabilize the object by gently placing gauze around it
- Place roller bandages around the object
- Shield the eye and bandages with a paper or plastic cup, making sure the shield is not in contact with the object
- Keep the shield in place by placing a roller bandage around the head and the shield.

The injured person should follow up with their medical doctor to check if their tetanus vaccine is up to date. **Tetanus** is caused by bacteria and can enter the body when the skin is cut by a rusted nail, a sharp object, or an animal bite. Tetanus bacteria is a poison that causes painful paralysis of the muscles, attacks the nervous system, and can be fatal if not treated immediately.

GENERAL CARE FOR MINOR OPEN WOUNDS

- Use disposable gloves
- Apply direct pressure to the wound until bleeding is controlled
- Gently wash the wound with soap and water and pat dry with a clean cloth
- Cover the wound with a sterile dressing and secure it in place with a bandage. The dressing absorbs blood and helps prevent further infection. Bandages help control bleeding, protect the injured site from infection, and provide support
- When applying a bandage, ensure it is not too tight by checking the extremities for color, warmth, and feeling

CARE FOR CHEEK INJURIES

Cheek injuries are treated the same way as minor open wounds.

- If the cheek is bleeding on the inside of the mouth, place a dressing on the inside of the cheek, and maintain pressure. You may have to add a dressing outside the cheek if it is bleeding
- Keep the person in a seated position leaning slightly forward, so blood is not swallowed
- Remove the object by gently pulling it in the same direction in which it entered the tissue
- In the case of an embedded object, **do not remove it. Instead**, call 911. The only exceptions are when

the embedded object is in the cheek, and blood may compromise breathing, or if the embedded object makes it challenging to give CPR

CARE FOR EYE INJURIES

In case of dirt, sand, or another small foreign body or chemical in the eye, try to flush it out with continuous flashing water. Ensure the affected eye is below the non-affected eye to prevent contamination to the other eye.

CARE FOR NOSE BLEED

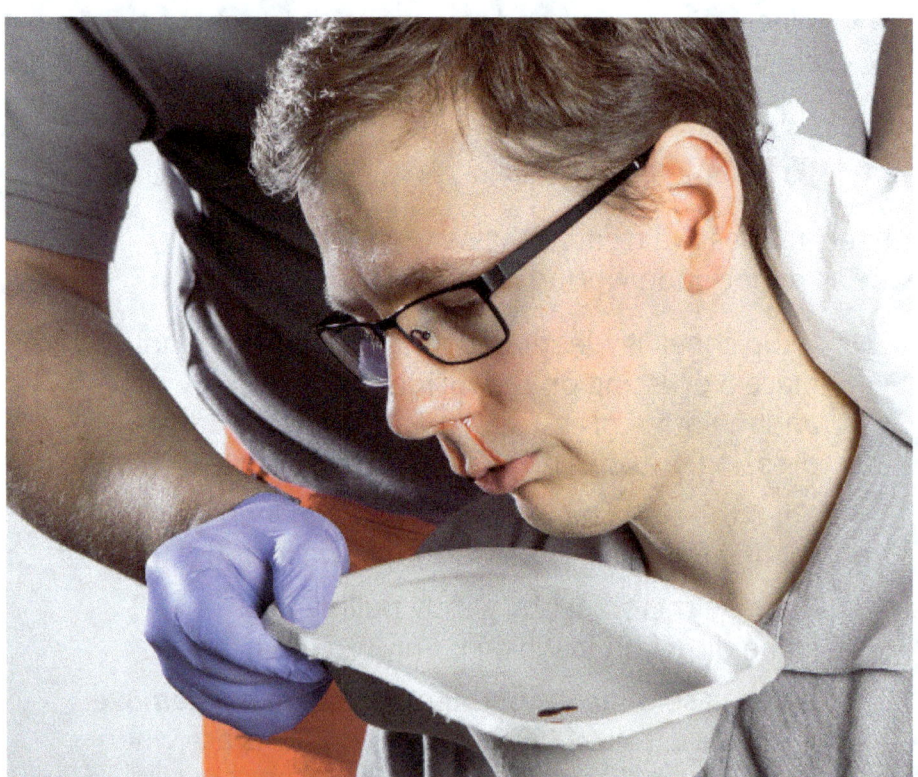

- Have the person sit with their head slightly leaning forward
- Pinch the nose for about 10 minutes
- Apply ice to the bridge of the nose if the bleeding continues

INFECTIONS

Any break in the skin is a potential risk for infection. Washing minor wounds with soap and a large amount of running water is essential. This will help flush away debris or germs.

SIGNS OF INFECTION

- Itchiness on or around the injury
- Inflammation that makes the wound become swollen and red
- Oozing of pus
- Fever or chills

If a sign of infection appears, clean the wound in warm water and apply an antibacterial ointment. If the person has a fever, chills, or gets worse, have them see a medical doctor.

GENERAL CARE FOR MAJOR OPEN WOUNDS

- Call 911
- Wear disposable gloves and protective eyewear

- Apply pressure directly to the wound using a dressing until the bleeding stops
- Apply a bandage over the dressing to maintain the pressure on the wound
- Add more bandages if blood soaks through. Never remove the soaked bandages.
- Have the person rest in the most comfortable position
- Monitor the person for changes in levels of consciousness, breathing, or skin color
- Keep the person from getting too cold or hot
- Wash your hands with soap and warm water

Special Situation: punctured chest
- Call 911
- Wear disposable gloves and protective eyewear
- In case of a punctured chest, instead of applying pressure, cover the wound with an occlusive dressing that does not let air pass through. You can use a plastic bag or folded cloth if no bag is available
- Tape the occlusive dressing in place, leaving one corner open. The opening will allow the air to escape with each exhale
- Have the person rest in the most comfortable position
- Monitor the person for changes in levels of consciousness, breathing, or skin color
- Keep the person from getting too cold or hot
- Wash your hands with soap and warm water

Special Situation: Abdominal Injuries

If the injury is severe, abdominal organs may be visible or protruding.

- Call 911
- Wear disposable gloves
- Do not apply pressure or try to push the organs back in. Instead, remove clothing from the injured area. Then, loosely cover the area with a clean dressing
- Cover the dressing with plastic wrap
- Use a blanket or towel to maintain warmth
- Keep the person from getting cold or hot

CLOSED WOUNDS

- Place a plastic bag with ice on the wound as soon as possible to reduce pain and swelling. Make sure there is a cloth between the wound and the bag prevents burns.
- Keep the ice pack on for 20 minutes, then remove it for 20 minutes. Alternate 20 minutes on and 20 minutes off.
- Elevate the limb

Call 911 if:

- The pain is too severe to move the limb
- You suspect the injury is serious and needs immediate medical attention
- The abdomen is distended
- The injured person vomits blood, shows changes in his/her level of consciousness, or becomes unconscious

BURNS

Heat, chemicals, electricity, or radiation can cause burns.

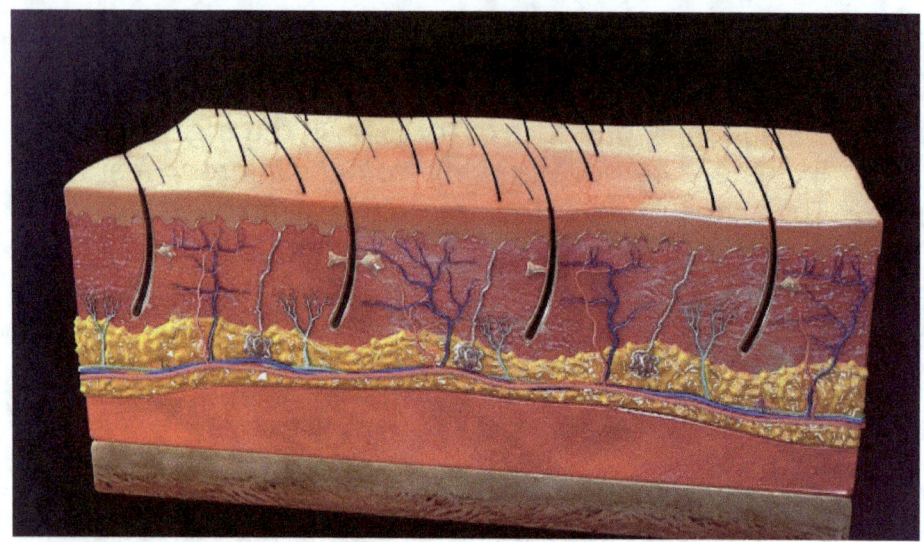

Superficial or **first-degree burns** cause the top layer of the skin to turn red and swollen. Within a week, the skin will heal completely with no scarring.

Partial-thickness burns or **second-degree burns** have the same symptoms as first-degree burns

- but may also have open or closed blisters filled with clear fluid. They may take several weeks to heal and can cause scarring.

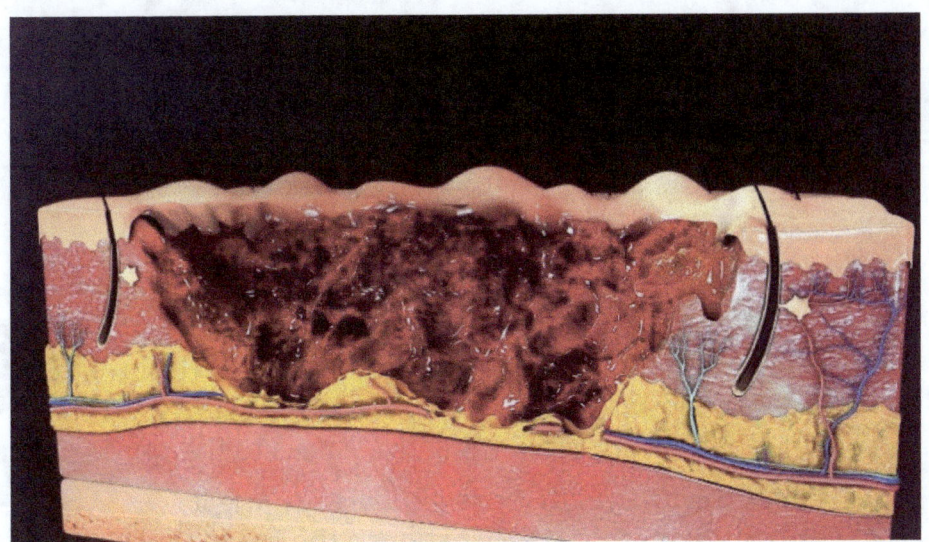

Third-degree burn

Full-thickness or **third-degree burns** may cause the skin to turn brown or black. They can destroy all the layers of the skin, and the tissues underneath can appear white. These types of burns require medical care.

Call 911 if:

- The burn covers a large area of the body or more than one body part
- The burn involves the head, face, neck, genitals, hands, or feet
- The burn involves the airways, including the nose and mouth
- The burn was caused by chemicals, electricity, or an explosion
- The person has trouble breathing
- The person appears to have a second or third-degree burn

CARE FOR THERMAL BURNS

- Check the scene
- Obtain consent
- Remove the person from the source of the burn
- Check for life-threatening conditions
- Cool the burn with cold running water until the pain has lessened. Burning will continue for some time, even after the source of the burn has been removed. Remove clothing from the burn unless it sticks to the wound. Do not pull clothing that sticks to the burn.
- Cover the burn with loose gauze, ensuring it remains wet, so it doesn't stick to the injury.
- Comfort the person and keep the person from being too cold or hot.

DO NOT:

- Try to clean the burned area
- Put any ointment or oil on second or third-degree burns
- Break blisters

CARE FOR CHEMICAL BURNS

Chemical burns can be caused by household solutions such as the ones used to clean, for gardening, or for fixing things around the house. Chemical burns are also common in industrial settings. These chemicals will continue burning as long they remain in contact with the skin.

- Obtain consent
- Call the National Poison Control Center at 1(800) 222-1222. They are available 24/7

- Wear protective gloves, and avoid direct contact with the chemical
- Flush the chemical away by pouring running water on the affected area for 20 minutes. Avoid using water under pressure, such as specific hose settings, as the pressure can damage the skin
- If an eye gets in contact with a chemical, flush it with water for 20 minutes
- If the chemical is a powder, brush it off with a towel
- Remove and dispose of the clothing

CARE FOR ELECTRICAL BURNS

Electrical burns may cause heart dysfunction, heart arrest, bone fractures, or muscle spasms. In addition, the injured person may become unconscious, confused, and/or have trouble breathing. An electrical burn may also have a burn on the skin at the site of entrance as well as on the side of the exit of the electrical current.

- Never approach someone who got electrocuted until you are 100% sure they are no longer in contact with the power source
- Turn off the power if possible
- Call 911
- Care for electrical burns at both the entry and exit sites of the burn
- Prepare to give CPR in case the person stops breathing

LIGHTNING

Lightning can cause deafness, blindness, permanent nerve damage, and even death.

Rule: when you see lightning, count the time it takes to hear the thunder. If it's under 30 seconds, the thunderstorm is close and dangerous. As a general rule, lightning strikes the tallest structures, so ensure you are not the tallest in the area. . If possible:

- If you are outdoors during lightning, stay in your car
- Seek shelter under cover such as a safe covered building, but stay away from open structures such as gazebos or porches. Remain in the shelter for at least 30 minutes after the lightning flashes.
- Move away from elevated areas such as the top of a hill or mountain
- Do not shelter under an isolated tree as they attract lightning
- Get away from bodies of water such as pools, lakes, or rivers
- Do not lie flat on the ground; instead, try to have the least amount of contact with the ground. Crouch down with your head tucked and cover your ears

Remember, when caring for burns, or chemical injuries, always ensure your personal safety first and then follow the CHECK-CALL-CARE steps.

CHAPTER 9

MUSCULOSKELETAL INJURIES
Injuries to the Muscles and Bones

INTRODUCTION

The musculoskeletal system includes the muscles, bones, and connective tissues of the tendons and ligaments. Although very painful, injuries to the musculoskeletal system are rarely life-threatening; however, immediate care is essential to limit the risks of permanent severe disabilities.

This chapter will teach you how to provide first aid care for fractures, sprains, and strains.

LEARNING OBJECTIVES

After reading this chapter, you will be able to:

- Differentiate between an open and closed fracture
- Differentiate between a sprain, strain, fracture, and a dislocation

- Demonstrate basic care for someone with a musculoskeletal injury
- Describe the RICE treatment technique

Skeletal muscles are soft tissues allowing the bones to move by contracting and relaxing. Most of them are attached to bones by tendons, also called connective tissues.

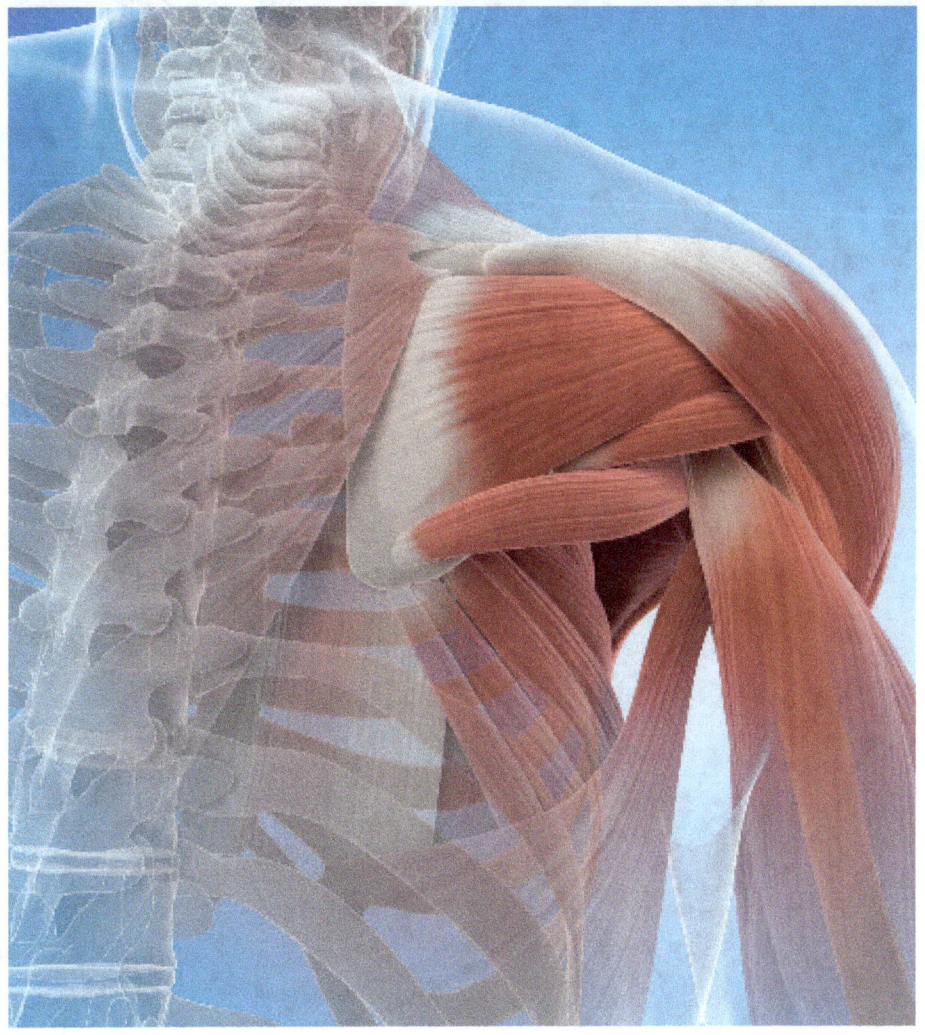

Other connective tissues, the ligaments, connect bones to bones, providing stability and support to the joints. Ligaments can tear partially or completely when a joint is forced beyond its normal range of motion due to an accident or blunt force.

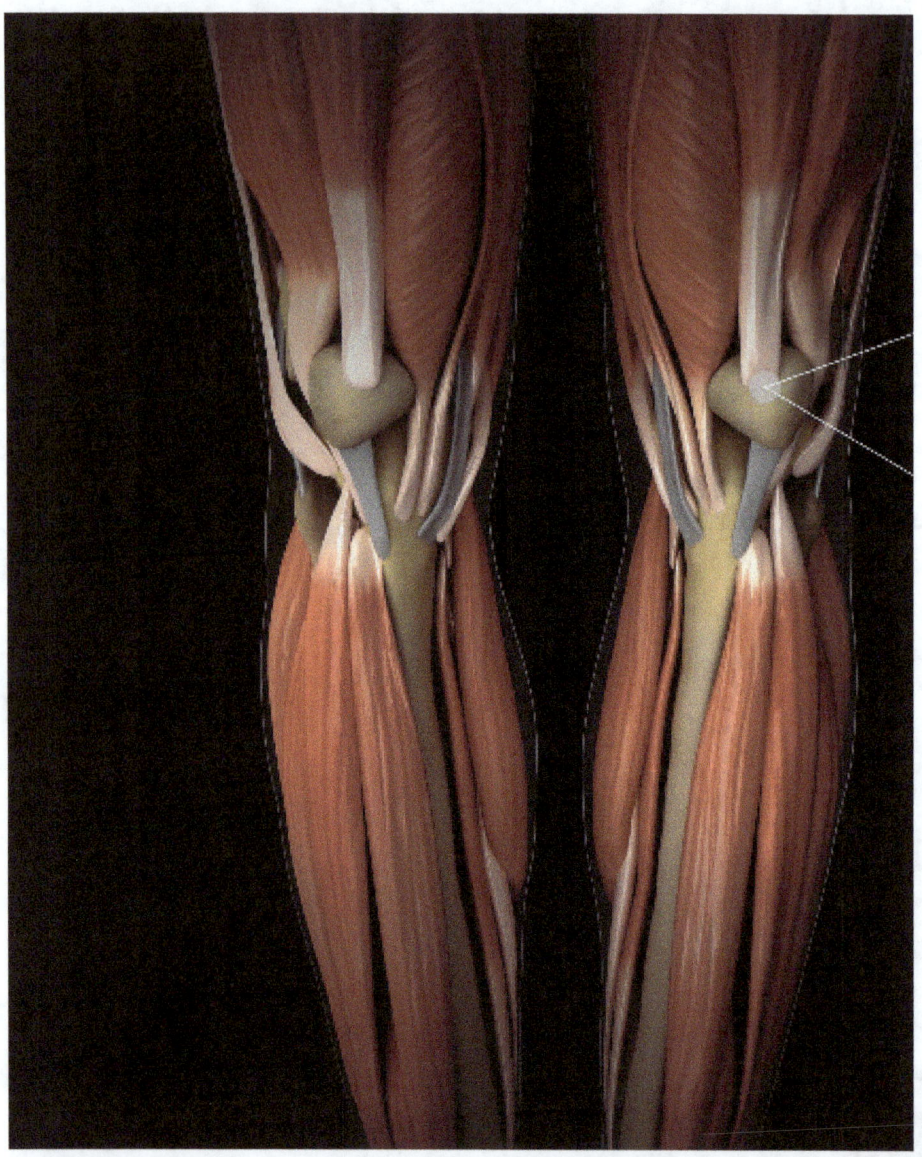

FRACTURES

Fractures refer to a bone that is broken, chipped, or cracked. Fractures can be classified as closed or open. In closed fractures, the skin remains intact. In open fractures, the broken bone breaks through the skin. Open fractures can be serious because blood loss can be severe, and infections can occur.

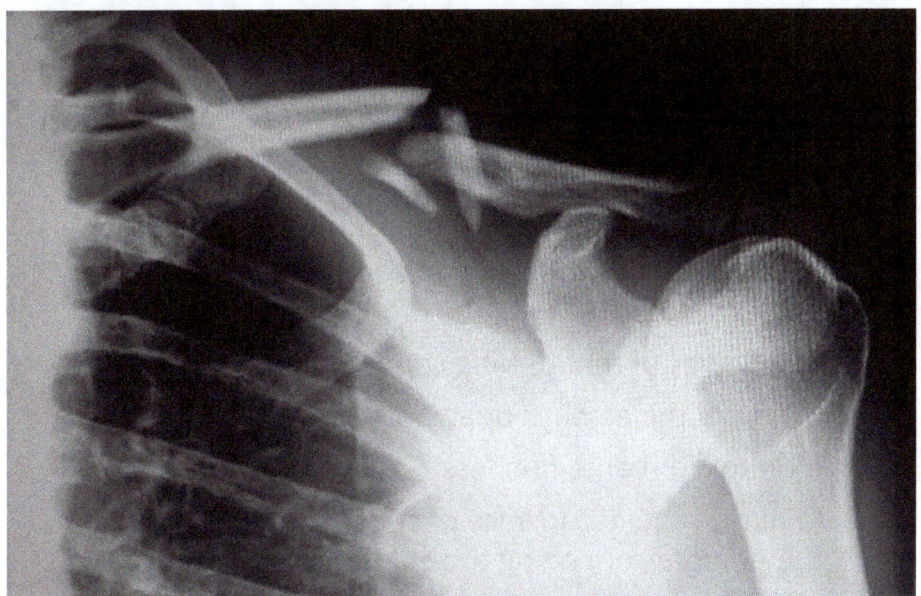

CARE FOR HEAD, NECK, AND SPINE INJURIES

Injuries to the head, neck, and spine are serious, and you should always call 911. These injuries can be life-threatening and cause breathing to stop. The care for neck and spinal cord injuries can vary from minor to life-threatening. If you suspect there is a chance of paralysis due to the nature of the accident, call 911, and prevent any movement. You should especially be concerned if there was a driving injury, a trauma force to the helmet, a fall from a height higher than the victim, or numbness, tingling, or loss of sensation in the extremities after an accident. If it is a minor injury, have the person consult their physician. In the meantime, apply a cold compress the first three days after the injury.

Steps to Take:

- Call 911
- Wear disposable gloves
- If the person is wearing a helmet, do not remove it unless it is necessary to access the airways
- Provide manual stabilization by supporting **the head in the position found** Keep the head and body as still as possible until the ambulance arrives
- Check for life-threatening conditions
- Maintain the airways open and monitor for breathing
- Monitor for consciousness
- Minimize the occurrence of shock by keeping the person from being too cold or too hot

CONCUSSIONS

Concussions result from a fall or blunt force to the head. It can temporarily cause reduced brain function.

SIGNS OF CONCUSSION:

- Temporary memory loss
- Mood change
- Confusion

- Nausea and vomiting
- Blurred vision and sensitivity to the light

CARE FOR CONCUSSIONS
- Reassure the person
- Monitor the person for changes in levels of consciousness or breathing
- Provide manual stabilization if necessary
- Keep the airways open

DISLOCATIONS

A dislocation occurs when the end of one bone moves out of socket. They are often the result of a violent blunt to the joint and usually include torn ligaments.

Once a joint has been dislocated, the joint becomes weak, and the injury can become chronic. The most common dislocations are the shoulder joints and fingers.

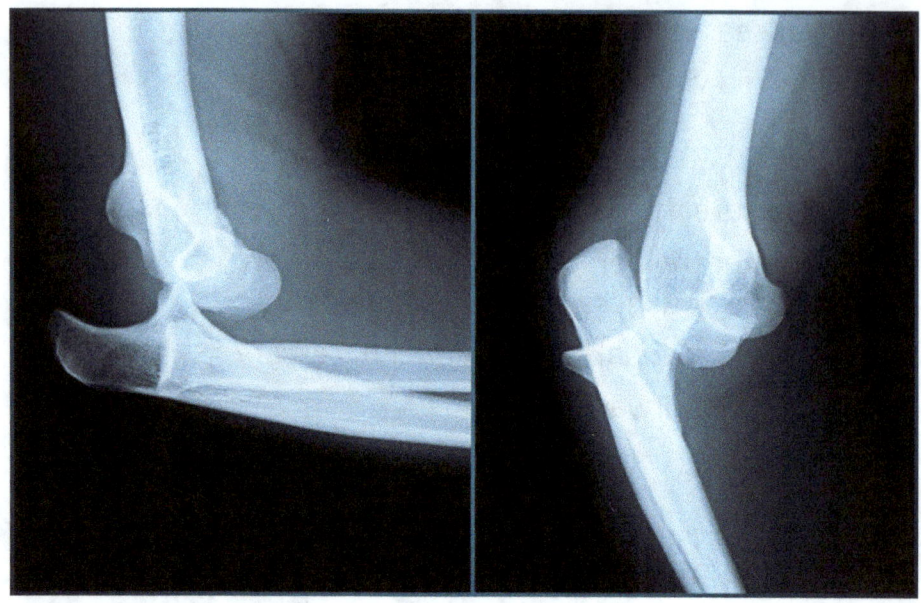

Elbow dislocation

SPRAINS

A sprain is a partial or complete tear of ligaments at a given joint. A sprain happens when excessive and sudden forces are applied to a joint that is forced beyond its normal range of motion. A severe sprain can be forceful enough to dislocate the joint.

A mild sprain only involves overstretching the ligaments. They result in momentary pain that subdues and heals quickly—for example, twisting your ankle while walking can result in a mild sprain. If the person sprains their ankle and is wearing shoes, do not remove them. The shoe will prevent blood pooling and reduce swelling.

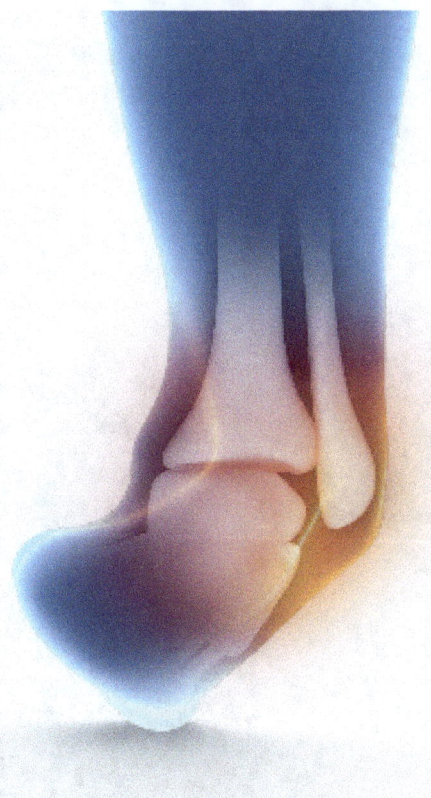

Moderate sprains involve the tearing of some of the ligaments of a joint. The pain is severe enough to make the person fall or stop all movement at the joint. Swelling and discoloration are common. After a sprain, the ligaments that have been overstretched and torn will not return to their original length. As a result, the joint will be less stable and at high risk of further sprains. Moderate sprains should be taken seriously because they will likely reoccur if not treated properly and promptly. They may take weeks to heal.

STRAINS

A strain or pull refers to a muscle or muscle group that has been overstretched or torn. It can result from a fall, overexertion while working out, using muscles improperly, an accident, or lifting a load that is too heavy.

Like sprains, strains can be very painful, especially in the back, neck, or thigh muscles.

SIGNS AND SYMPTOMS OF MUSCULAR SKELETAL INJURIES

The signs and symptoms of these injuries are often very similar, which may make it difficult to determine one injury from the other. The signs and symptoms include:

- Pain, discomfort
- Swelling
- Discoloration, bruising
- Numbness or tingling
- Deformity, bone sticking out
- Inability to use a body part
- Snapping sound

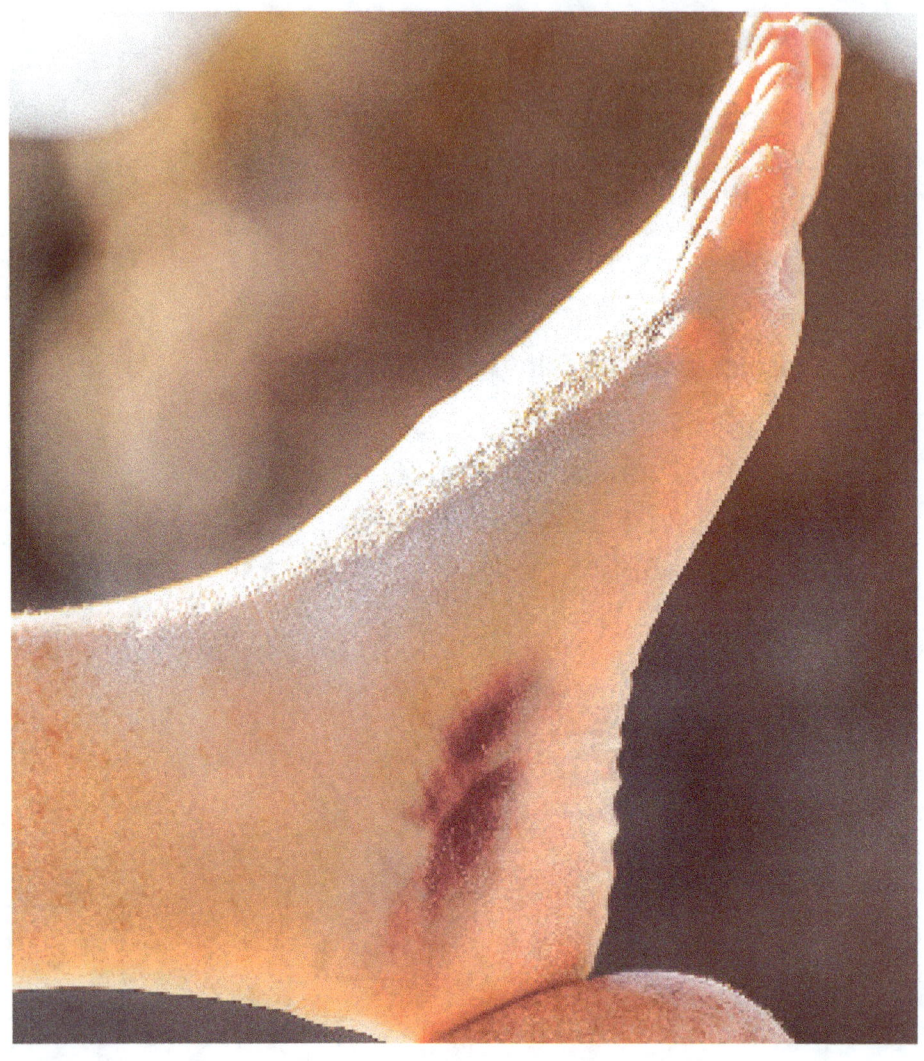

CARE FOR MUSCULOSKELETAL INJURIES

- Check the scene
- Obtain consent
- Reassure the person

- Keep the person in the most comfortable position
- Provide support for the injured area if it doesn't cause more pain
- The basic treatment steps for all musculoskeletal injuries involve using a technique called **RICE** (**R**est, **I**mmobilize, **C**old, **El**evate)

RICE TECHNIQUE

Rest

Rest is the most important thing to do when you first get injured. Rest will prevent further damage to the injured joint or limb and allow the body to start healing.

Immobilize

In the next chapter, you will learn how to splint an injured limb. **If you are waiting for an ambulance, do not immobilize the limb.**

Cold

Cold lessens the pain and reduces swelling and bleeding.

Make an ice pack by filling a plastic bag with water and ice, or use a bag of frozen vegetables. Do not place the ice pack directly in contact with the skin, as this could burn the skin. Instead, place gauze, paper towel, or cloth between the ice pack and the skin.

Keep the icepack on the injured limb for 20 minutes, then remove it for 20 minutes. Repeat the cycle of 20 minutes on and 20 minutes off throughout the day.

Elevate

Elevating the injured limb reduces swelling and prevents blood from pooling towards the injury. Only move an injured part if it does not cause further pain.

The **RICE** technique is the first step after an injury that is not severe. The second step is to follow up with a medical doctor immediately.

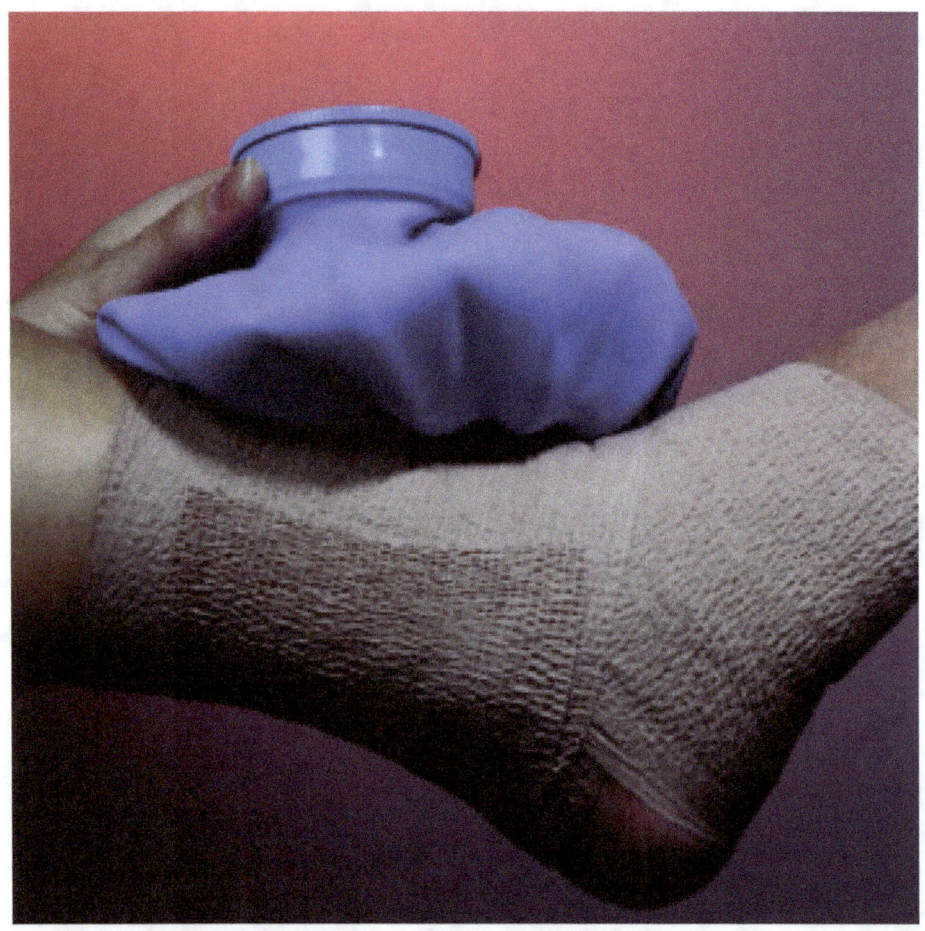

In the next chapter, you will learn how to splint an injured limb

SPLINTING

INTRODUCTION

This chapter outlines the techniques to splint an injured body part using improvised items available at the time of injury. Splinting is the process of immobilizing a limb before transporting a person to the hospital. The immobilization helps support the injured area and reduce pain.

LEARNING OBJECTIVES

After reading this chapter, you will be able to:

- Describe the purpose of splinting
- List the general steps to immobilize a limb
- List the signs of a fractured femur
- Demonstrate how to splint a finger, arm, ankle, and leg

GENERAL RULES FOR SPLINTING

- Only apply a splint if you are transporting the person to the hospital. For example, do not use a splint if you are waiting for an ambulance

- Only splint an injured area if it does not cause more harm or pain
- Keep the limb in the position found; do not try to straighten the limb
- Splint above and below the injury
- Care for open wounds before splinting
- Look at the non-injured extremity for circulation. Check the color, temperature, and sensation. Compare both limbs before and after splinting to make sure it is not too tight
- Elevate the injured area if it does not cause more pain

TYPES OF SPLINTS

SOFT SPLINT

Soft splints are made of soft cloth, towels, blankets, and pillows and can be used with slings and binders. **Sling and Binder** are a specific type of splint that uses a triangular cloth to provide support and immobilize the shoulder, arm, and elbow. Binders are a piece of fabric used to immobilize an injured arm against the body to provide more support and reduce pain. Binders can be used independently or with a binder to support the injured area.

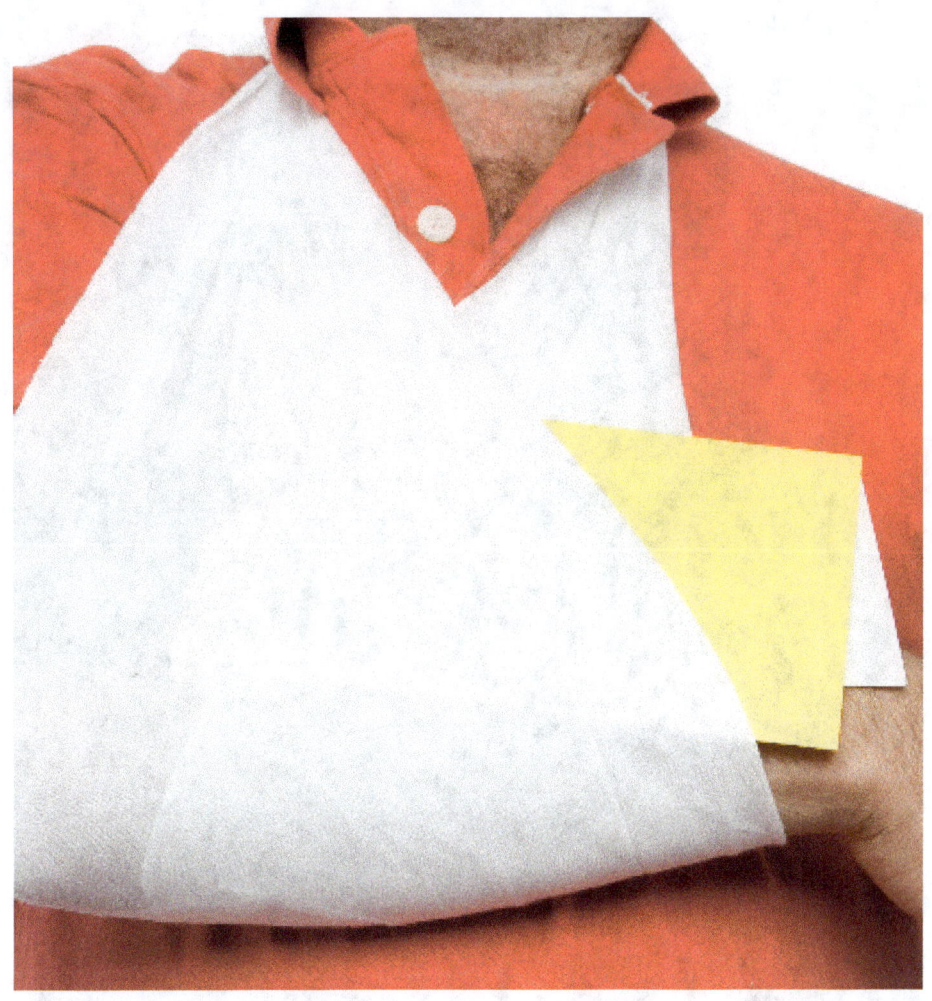
Soft Splint

RIGID SPLINT

A rigid splint is made of rigid materials such as cardboards, magazines, or any rigid object that is available such as a spoon, plastic, wood, or a ruler.

ANATOMICAL SPLINT

Anatomical Splint

An anatomical splint uses a non-injured body part to support the injured limb. For example, you can splint an injured finger against the rest of the fingers, or an injured leg against the non-injured leg.

It can be difficult to determine the nature and severity of an injury. For that reason, assume that it is serious. When splinting, focus on providing support and minimizing pain with whatever material you have available. Recall that you should not splint an injured limb if an ambulance is on its way..

CHAPTER 11

SUDDEN ILLNESSES

INTRODUCTION

This chapter teaches you how to recognize and care for sudden illnesses. Sudden illnesses can be chronic or happen unexpectedly. In an emergency sudden illness, it can be hard to determine the exact cause because symptoms can be very similar across illnesses. However, regardless of the cause, you can always help someone who is having a diabetic emergency, seizure, stroke, or who is fainting by following the steps outlined in this chapter.

LEARNING OBJECTIVES

After reading this chapter, you will be able to:

- List the signs for common sudden illnesses
- Describe the general guidelines for someone experiencing a sudden illness
- Demonstrate how to care for someone who faints
- Demonstrate how to care for someone who has a diabetic emergency
- Demonstrate how to care for someone who has a seizure

- Demonstrate how to care for someone who is having a stroke

GENERAL CARE FOR SUDDEN ILLNESSES

- Check the scene
- Obtain consent
- Ask the person if they want you to call 911
- Reassure and comfort the person
- Help the person to rest in the most comfortable position
- Assist with prescribed medication
- Monitor the person's level of consciousness and breathing
- Give care for the specific condition you found

CARE FOR FAINTING

Fainting is a momentary loss of consciousness due to reduced blood flow to the brain. In most cases, when the person collapses, blood goes back to the brain and allows the person to regain consciousness on their own. There are usually no serious consequences, and caring for the person is simple:

- Place the person on their back
- Check for breathing
- Loosen up tight clothes around the neck
- Roll the person on their side if they vomit
- Call 911 if you suspect the fall may have caused an injury

DIABETIC EMERGENCY

Diabetes is a chronic illness in which the pancreas either doesn't produce insulin or doesn't produce enough insulin. Sometimes the body cannot use insulin properly, and blood sugar levels become too high. For example, blood sugar levels rise when the food you eat is broken down. High blood sugar levels trigger the pancreas to release the hormone insulin. Insulin is necessary to move blood sugar from the bloodstream to the cells for energy. Without insulin, sugar remains in the blood, causing high blood sugar. People with type 1 diabetes do not produce any insulin. Instead, they rely on insulin shots and medications for the duration of their lives. Type 2 diabetes develops later in life, resulting from poor diet and lack of exercise. People with type 2 diabetes produce insulin but not in adequate amounts. Diet, weight loss, and exercise provide the best outcome for people with type 2 diabetes who want to reduce their medication intake under the supervision of a medical doctor.

Diabetes Risk Factors

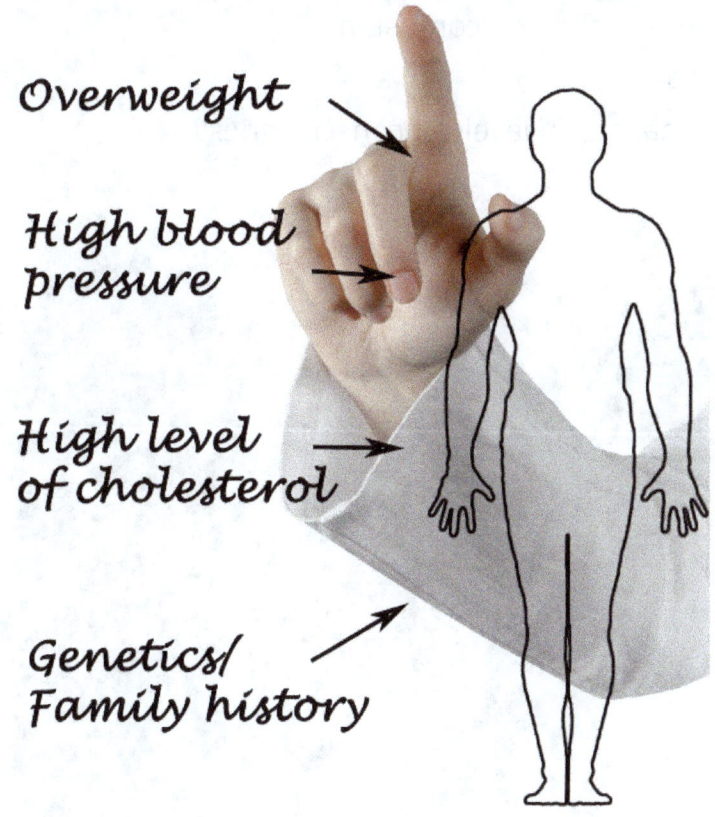

- Overweight
- High blood pressure
- High level of cholesterol
- Genetics/Family history

People with diabetes can suddenly suffer a diabetic emergency if blood sugar levels are too high or too low. However, first aid care for diabetic emergencies is the same regardless of whether blood sugar is too high or too low.

SIGNS OF DIABETIC EMERGENCY

- Feeling and looking ill
- Clammy skin

- Changes in mood, suddenly becoming moody
- Changes in levels of consciousness
- Headache and confusion
- Fast heart rate
- Changes in levels of consciousness

People with diabetes may suddenly have a diabetic emergency if their blood sugar levels become too high or too low. Elevated blood sugar levels can lead to a severe emergency resulting in a seizure, diabetic coma, or death.

When blood sugar levels are too low, it can lead to insulin shock or death. This can happen when people take too much insulin, over exercise, skip a meal, or are under high levels of stress.

CARE FOR DIABETIC EMERGENCIES

Both types of diabetic emergencies (low and high blood sugar levels) are treated the same way:

- Check the scene
- Obtain consent
- If the person is conscious and has their medication with them, help them take it, but do not administer insulin to them. Instead, let them do it on their own
- If the person is conscious, but does not have their medication with them, give them sugar in the form of fruit juice, non-diet soft drink, or milk (7 oz for children and 17 oz for adults.

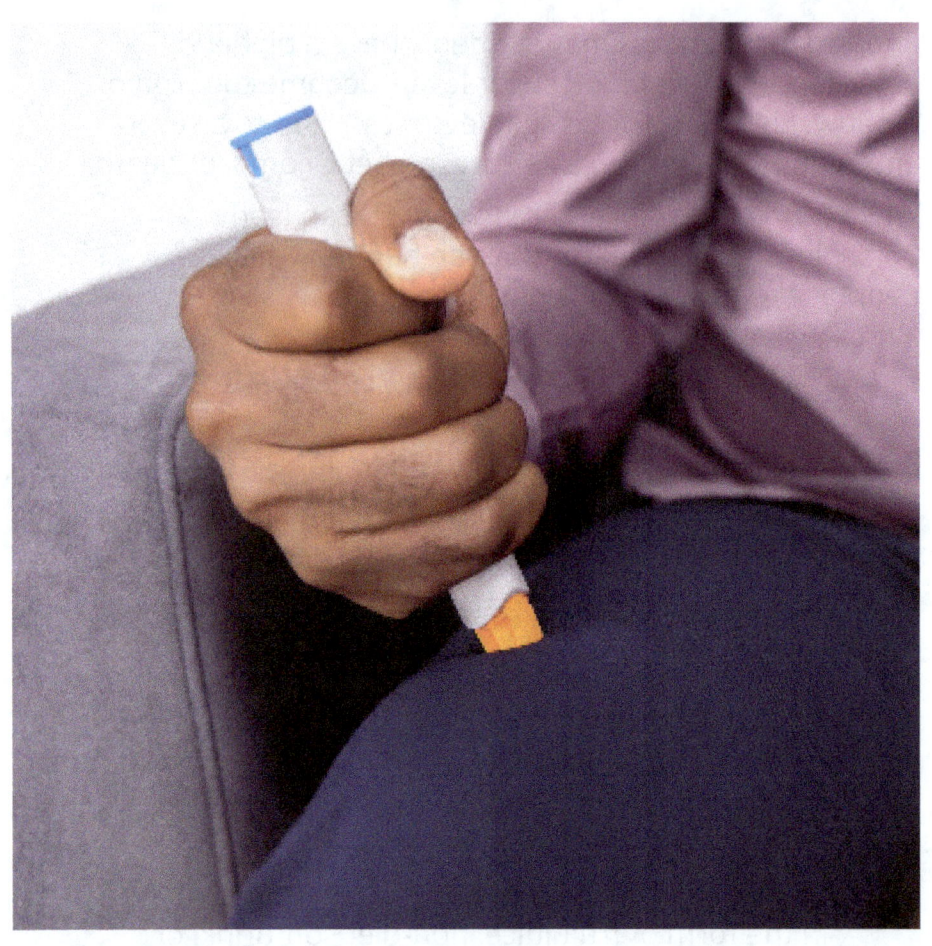

Call 911 if:

- The person is unconscious
- The person is conscious but can't drink or eat anything
- You don't have anything sweet to drink or eat to give them
- The symptoms have not improved after 5 minutes. Ask the person if it's ok to call an ambulance

CARE FOR SEIZURES

Seizures are sudden abnormal electrical disturbances in the brain. They can be due to injuries, infections, diseases, or fever. Seizures can sometimes happen unnoticeably or be very serious and lead to the person becoming unconscious with uncontrollable movements and convulsions. When seizures become chronic, we use the term **epilepsy** to describe the disorder.

During seizures, the person may release urine and have a bowel movement, feeling embarrassed when they regain consciousness. It is essential to provide privacy by having onlookers walk away. Have one close friend or family member stay close to the person after they regain consciousness for reassurance.

- Move furniture or object away from the person to avoid injury
- Protect the person's head by placing a pillow or another soft object under their head to protect it from hitting the floor
- Let the seizure run its course

Call 911 if:

- This is a first seizure
- The seizure lasts more than 5 minutes
- The person is having repeated seizures
- The person is a child, pregnant, or an elderly
- The person does not regain consciousness
- The person is diabetic

STROKE

A stroke happens when blood flow to the brain is interrupted. It can be caused by a blood clot (**thrombus**) in the brain or a ruptured artery in the brain. In addition, high blood pressure, **atherosclerosis** (a buildup of fat, cholesterol, and other deposits), defective artery walls, or a tumor can rupture an artery. Strokes can permanently damage the brain, and lead to disability or death.

Lifestyle is the most critical factor you have under your control to reduce your risk of having a stroke. A healthy diet and regular exercise can lower your chances of heart attacks and strokes. Risk factors include high blood pressure, cholesterol, diabetes, and heart diseases. Other factors such as gender, age, and family history are beyond your control.

SIGNS OF A STROKE

- Droopiness
- Weakness in one side of the body
- Loss of coordination and balance
- Slurred speech
- Blurred vision
- Incontinence
- Dizziness, confusion, altered levels of consciousness
- Sudden, extremely severe headache

CARE FOR A STROKE

We use the acronym **FAST** to remember what signs to look for when we suspect someone is experiencing a stroke. It is also important to get medical care as soon as possible if you suspect the person is having or has had a stroke:

- Check the scene
- Obtain consent
- Have the person sit in a comfortable position
- Assess the person's condition using the FAST technique:
    - **F**ace: the face may be partially paralyzed and droopy or drooling. The person may be unable to smile on both sides of the mouth. Check by asking them to smile.
    - **A**rm: there may be a weakness in one arm or leg. Check by asking the person to extend both arms and to resist when you apply equal pressure over and under both arms
    - **S**lurred speech: ask the person to repeat a sentence
    - **T**ime: act quickly if the person is experiencing the above symptoms. Take note of the time when the symptoms first occurred and report it to the medical personnel. Call 911
- Be prepared to give CPR
- Monitor the person
- Reassure the person
- Do not give them anything to drink or eat

Depending on the situation and promptness of care, a person can recover completely or have permanent damage.

GENERAL CARE FOR POISONING

Poisons are substances that can cause injury, illnesses, or death once they enter the body. Poisons can enter the body in five ways: ingested, inhaled, absorbed by the skin, or injected into the body. The severity of the injury depends on the type of poison, the amount of poison, how it entered the body, how long it has been in the body, the person's size, age, and heart. In case of poisoning, follow the **CHECK-CALL-CARE** steps:

- Check the scene
- Obtain consent
- If possible, remove the source of poisoning
- Check for life-threatening conditions
- Look for the container of the poison and keep it
- Call the National Control Center Hotline (1-800-222-1222)
- If the poison was absorbed by the skin, rinse the affected area with water for 20 minutes
- For injected poisons such as insects or animals bites, place an icepack on the affected area to reduce pain
- When a person has ingested a poison, do not induce vomiting unless instructed to do so by the National Poison Control Center Hotline or a medical professional

Call 911 if:

- The person has trouble breathing or is not breathing
- The person is unconscious

- The person has seizures, severe headaches, or slurred speech
- The person is vomiting blood
- The person has chest pain, abdominal pain, or is passing blood in stool or urine.

ALLERGIC REACTIONS

Any source of poison can cause an allergic reaction, also known as **anaphylaxis**. Medication, poison, insect bites, stings, or contact with certain chemicals can cause an allergic reaction. Anaphylaxis is a life-threatening condition that needs to be cared for immediately.

SIGNS OF ANAPHYLAXIS

- Problems breathing, wheezing, or shortness of breath
- Swelling of the face, throat, or tongue
- Hives or a rash
- Feeling dizzy or confused
- Feeling pressure on the chest
- Shock

GENERAL CARE FOR ALLERGIC REACTION

- Check the scene
- Obtain consent
- Call 911

- Check the person for life-threatening conditions
- If the person is conscious, try to find out what happened. Interview the person to find out if they have allergies, medication, or medical conditions. Try to find out what happened and how they feel. If the person has an epinephrine auto-injector, help them access it and help them with the injection

CARE FOR BEE STINGS

Some people are allergic to bee stings. Their throat and mouth may swell when stung, blocking the airways and making breathing difficult.

If someone gets stung by a bee:

- Check the scene
- Obtain consent
- Ask the person if they are allergic to bees. If so, ask them if they have an epinephrine auto-injector. If they don't have any medication with them, try to get some Benadryl to reduce the inflammation
- Call 911
- Reassure the person
- Remove the stinger using a credit card to gently scrape off the stinger. Do not use tweezers because they will push the venom inside the body.
- Be prepared to give CPR.

If they are not allergic or you do not notice any allergic reaction, reassure the person.

- Use a credit card to scrape off the stinger gently
- Wash the affected area with soap
- Apply a clean compress or gauze

Keep all medication and household items with their labels on and in their original containers. Do not use empty containers for other products. All medications or chemicals should be out of reach of children.

When someone suddenly becomes ill, it can be challenging to determine what is happening. Sometimes, the ill person may not know what is happening either. The key is to recognize the symptoms of sudden illness. As a lay responder, your role is to provide first aid care the best you can, while more advanced care can take over regardless of the cause of illness.

CARE FOR OPIOIDS OVERDOSE

- Call 911
- Naloxone should be administered to someone who shows symptoms of an opioid overdose. It can be given as a nasal spray or into the muscle. Repeat every two to three minutes.

CHAPTER

HEAT AND COLD-RELATED EMERGENCIES

INTRODUCTION

In this chapter, you will learn how to recognize and care for heat- and cold-related emergencies. Heat- and cold-related emergencies are affected by the age and health of the person, as well as humidity levels, wind, and other environmental conditions.

LEARNING OBJECTIVES

After reading this chapter, you will be able to:

- List the signs of heat emergencies
- Describe the step to care for dehydration
- Describe the care for heat cramps
- Describe the care for heat exhaustion
- Describe the care for heat stroke
- Explain the steps to prevent heat-related emergencies

- Explain the steps to prevent cold-related emergencies
- Demonstrate how to care for frostbites
- Describe how to care for hypothermia

Both heat- and cold-related emergencies can progress quickly and become life-threatening. The average body temperature is 98.6 degrees Fahrenheit (37 degrees Celsius), and to maintain life, it must be kept between 97.7F and 99 degrees Fahrenheit (36.5 and 37.2 Celsius).

HEAT-RELATED EMERGENCIES

Hot temperatures can cause damage to the organs and brain. Your body attempts to stay cool by sweating. However, heat is released when sweat evaporates and cools the body. When this is not enough, the body may suffer a heat-related emergency going from dehydration to heat stroke. Recognizing the symptoms will help you determine how serious the situation is.

SIGNS OF DEHYDRATION

Dehydration happens when fluid intakes are inadequate, or when people vomit or have diarrhea. Young children and older adults are at a much higher risks of dying from dehydration.

- Weakness, fatigue
- Dizziness
- Dry lips and dry mouth
- Headache
- Irritability

- Excessive thirst
- Nausea
- Disorientation
- Lack of tears
- Dark urine
- Loss of appetite
- Unconsciousness

CARE FOR DEHYDRATION

- Have the person drink fluids as soon as you notice the signals to help replace the fluid lost
- Have the person drink slowly to prevent vomiting

HEAT CRAMPS

Heat cramps commonly happen after an intense exercise session in a warm or hot environment. As a result, the person may start experiencing muscle cramps and spasms.

- Muscle spasms
- Muscle cramps
- Moist skin

CARE FOR HEAT CRAMPS

- Remove the person from the heat. Move the person to a shaded area or in a location with air conditioning.
- Give fluid replacement
- Massage the affected muscles

HEAT EXHAUSTION

Heat exhaustion is caused by fluid loss through sweating.

SIGNS OF HEAT EXHAUSTION

- Muscle cramps
- Heavy sweating
- Weakness, exhaustion
- Dizziness
- Shallow breathing
- Cool, moist skin
- Pale or flushed skin
- Headaches
- Nausea

CARE FOR HEAT EXHAUSTION

- Move the person to a cooler location
- Remove tight clothing
- Give cold drinks or fluids
- Monitor the person

If the condition doesn't improve, call 911. If the condition worsens, it can lead to heat stroke, which is life-threatening.

HEAT STROKES

Heat stroke is the most severe heat-related emergency and is a life-threatening emergency that is usually caused by heat exhaustion that was not cared for. With heat strokes, the body stops sweating and, as a result, can no longer release excess body heat. Body temperature keeps rising and can damage the brain, kidneys, and heart, leading to coma and eventually death. Heat strokes affect infants, the elderly, or people with chronic medical conditions who may not have access to air conditioning. Athletes can also develop heatstroke under high temperatures and humidity due to intense physical activity.

SIGNS OF A HEAT STROKE

- Rapid breathing
- Red or flushed skin
- Dizziness
- Nausea or vomiting
- Throbbing headaches
- High blood pressure
- Confusion
- Changes in levels of consciousness
- Seizures

CARE FOR HEAT STROKE

- Call 911

- Cool the entire person with cold water, either in a bath or with ice-cold towels over the whole body
- Be prepared to perform CPR

COLD-RELATED EMERGENCIES

When the body gets cold, blood vessels in the extremities start to constrict. As a result, blood flow is redirected to the vital organs to keep them warm. If the body's temperature keeps getting colder, it starts shivering in an attempt to maintain body temperature. The quick muscle contractions help produce heat and warm the body. There are two types of cold-related emergencies: *frostbites* and *hypothermia*.

Frostbites occur when the skin or tissues in the fingers, toes, ears, and nose freezes due to exposure to cold temperatures. Severe frostbites can cause loss of the damaged body part.

SIGNS OF FROSTBITES

- Lack of sensation in the fingers, toes, ears, or nose
- Cold skin
- Waxy discolored skin color. When deep tissues are affected, skin color can turn black
- Blisters

CARE FOR FROSTBITES

- Bring the person to warm conditions as soon as possible
- Remove wet clothing

- Gently warm the affected area with skin-to-skin contact, a blanket, or a heat source. **Do not rub** the affected area as it can damage the skin
- Provide warm liquid
- Place fingers or toes into warm water (105 degrees) for 20-30 minutes. Test that the water temperature is warm but not uncomfortable
- Gently and loosely place gauze between and around their fingers or toes
- Monitor and keep the person warm
- Call 911

DO NOT:

- Rub the affected area as it may further damage the skin
- Break blisters
- Warm up a frozen body part that may refreeze before getting medical help

SIGNALS OF HYPOTHERMIA

Hypothermia happens when the body is unable to maintain normal body temperature. The drop in temperature leads to abnormal heart rhythm and eventually death.

- Initially, the person will shiver, but in more advanced cases, shivering may stop
- Weakness or apathy
- Confusion, unresponsive, memory loss
- Slurred speech
- Loss of coordination
- Numbness

- Changes in levels of consciousness

CARE FOR HYPOTHERMIA

- Call 911
- Remove the person from the cold
- Remove wet clothing
- Progressively warm the body with blankets and bring the person close to a source of heat
- Provide warm drink or food if the person is alert
- Monitor the person's levels of consciousness
- Be prepared to perform CPR
- Do NOT rub or massage the extremities

You can minimize the risks of heat and cold-related emergencies by wearing appropriate clothing when spending time outdoors. Wear light and loose clothes in hot temperatures and layers of clothing in cold temperatures. Avoid being outdoors during the hottest or coldest part of the day, and reduce the amount of time you spend outdoors when temperatures are extremes. Drink plenty of fluid and adjust your exercise intensity and duration in hot or cold weather conditions.

CHAPTER

EMERGENCY CHILDBIRTH

INTRODUCTION

In this chapter, you will learn how to identify the different stages of labor, how to help assist with the delivery of a newborn in case of an emergency, how to care for the newborn and the mother after delivery, and how to handle complications until medical care arrives.

LEARNING OBJECTIVES

After reading this chapter, you will be able to:

- Describe the steps to prepare the mother for an emergency delivery
- List the materials and supplies used to assist an emergency delivery
- Describe the steps needed to assist with delivering a newborn
- Describe how to care for the newborn
- Describe how to care for the mother after delivery

Emergency Childbirth 147

- Identify complications that may occur during an emergency delivery and how to care for them

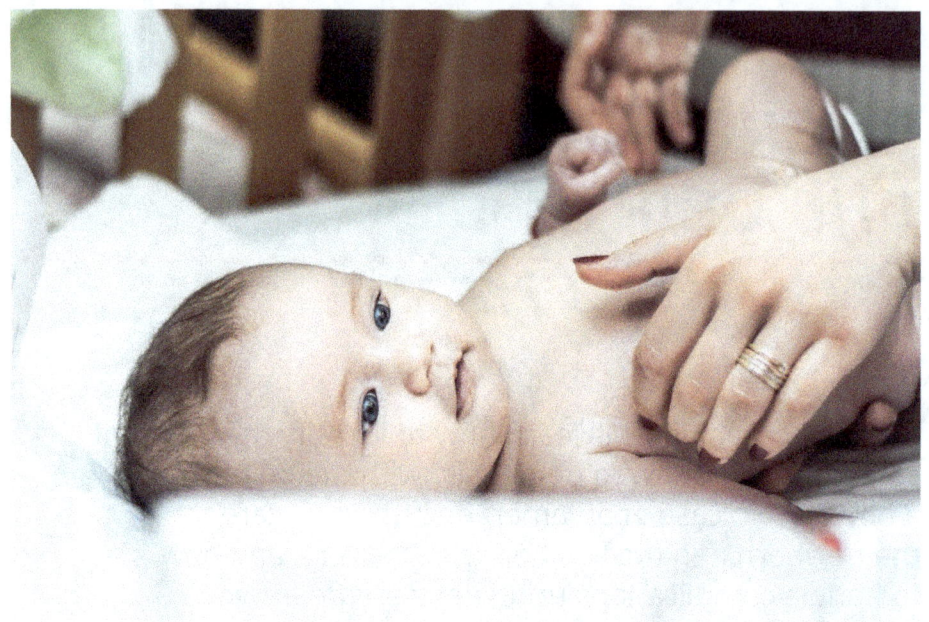

STAGES OF LABOR

When a mother is getting ready to deliver her baby, she goes into labor that can last between 12 to 24 hours on average for first-time mothers. Labor is characterized by contractions of the uterus that allow the cervix to dilate. Once the cervix is fully dilated, the newborn can pass through the birth canal and be born.

Labor has four stages:

STAGE 1-DILATION

Dilation begins with the first contraction until the cervix is fully dilated. Contractions start gently and increase in intensity, then lessen over 30 to 60 seconds. Initially, contractions are far apart but progressively get closer and closer together and last longer. When contractions are about 3-5 minutes apart, the mother should be transported to the hospital. At times, this is not possible, or the contractions suddenly get too close together to go to the hospital, and the mother may have her baby before getting medical assistance.

STAGE 2-EXPULSION

The cervix is fully dilated during this stage, and contractions are powerful. They last between 45 to 90 seconds. The pressure becomes intense, and the mother begins to push the baby through the birth canal. Blood, stool, urine, and vomit are common occurrences during delivery. Under normal circumstances, the baby is born head first.

STAGE THREE-PLACENTA DELIVERY

About 30 minutes after the baby is born, the placenta dislodges from the uterus wall and is released from the body.

STAGE 4-STABILIZATION

The uterus contracts to help the healing process.

EMERGENCY DELIVERY ASSISTANCE

CHECKING THE MOTHER

- Call 911

- Ask questions to determine in what stage of labor the mother is in:
    - Is this your first pregnancy? This is important to know because labor is much longer with first pregnancies than in the following ones
    - Time how far apart the contractions are. If they are less than 3 minutes apart, it may be too late to transport the mother to the hospital, and you will have to assist with the delivery
    - Did your water break? This can be characterized by a sudden gush of fluid from the vagina and indicates birth is very close
    - Did you have a bloody show or pink discharge from the vagina? This happens on the first onset of cervix dilation, indicating birth is imminent
    - Do you feel an urge to push or defecate? This is another signal that birth is about to happen. Do not allow the mother to go to the bathroom as she may deliver her newborn while on the toilet.

Once you have determined the mother is about to deliver, reassure the mother.

- Help her focus on inhaling and exhaling slowly
- Comfort her
- Lay clean sheets, blankets, or paper towels on the surface where the mother will be delivering her baby
- Provide privacy

Try to gather:

- a bulb syringe to suction the baby's mouth and nose after birth
- a plastic bag to hold the placenta
- extra pads and towels to catch the newborn and wipe the mother
- gauze
- gloves or plastic bags to cover your hands
- protective glasses

DELIVERING THE INFANT

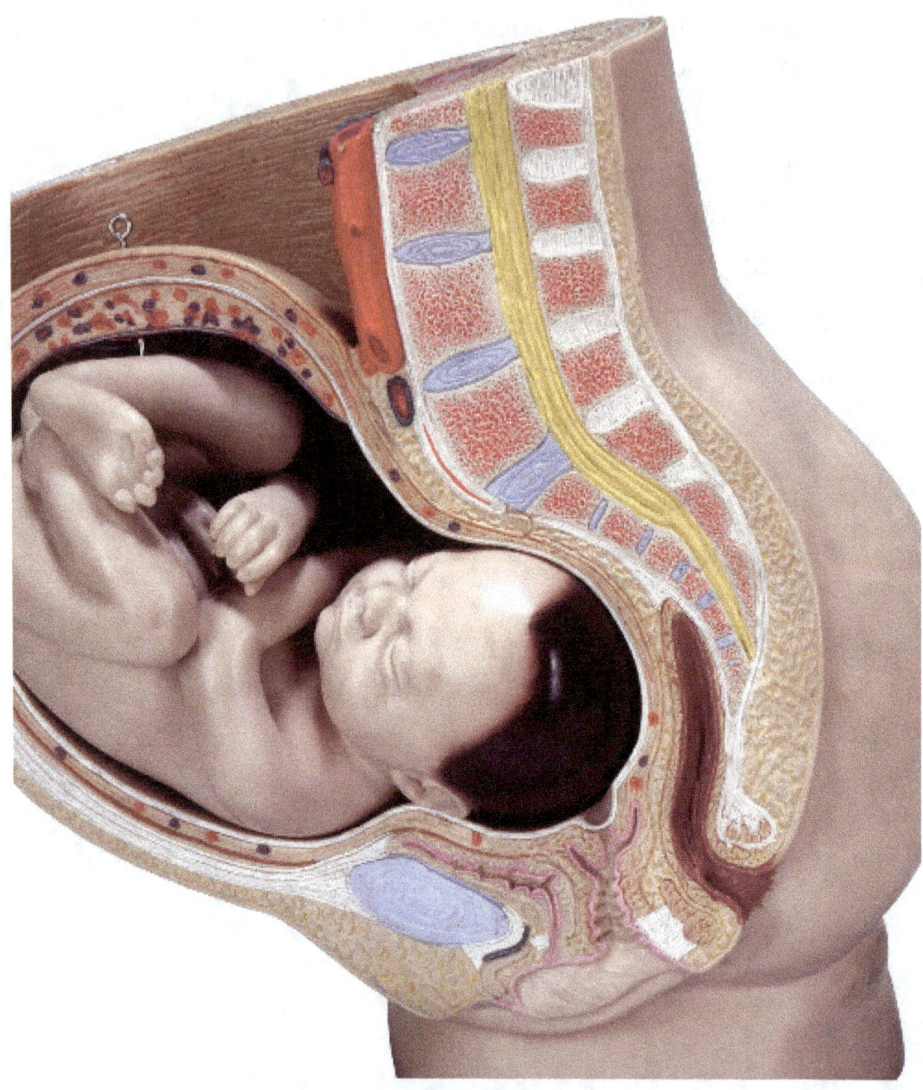

- Wear disposable gloves or a plastic bag around your hands
- Wear protective glasses if available
- Cover your clothes to protect them from bodily fluids

- Have the mother lay on her back over the towels with her legs wide open
- Have her upper back slightly raised
- Once crowning starts, and you see the head of the infant, support the head with your hands, then very gently apply light pressure over the top of the infant's head.
- Instruct the mother to stop pushing to prevent forceful delivery and tearing of the vagina
- Allow the newborn's head to turn sideways and support it with both hands
- Slide one finger along the newborn's neck to ensure the umbilical cord is not wrapped around the neck. If the umbilical cord is around the neck, slide it over the head or over one shoulder once the shoulder is out.
- Allow the infant to come out without pulling
- Guide one shoulder out at a time
- Place the newborn on the towel

NEVER DO THE FOLLOWING
- Pull on the newborn
- Allow the mother to use the bathroom during the delivery
- Place your fingers inside the mother
- The placenta will remain attached to the newborn's umbilical cord. Therefore, do not pull the umbilical cord.

CARING FOR THE NEWBORN AND THE MOTHER

- Use the syringe to suction the mouth and then the nose of the newborn. Use gauze if you do not have a syringe
- If the newborn is not crying, rub the lower back or flick your finger on the bottom of the baby's foot
- If the baby doesn't cry, begin CPR
- After the newborn starts crying, place him or her on the mother's abdomen to begin nursing. Breastfeeding stimulates contraction of the uterus and healing from the delivery
- When the placenta is expelled, place it in a plastic bag or towel, but do not detach it from the newborn
- Monitor the condition of both the mother and newborn

Bulb syringe

COMPLICATIONS DURING DELIVERY
BREECH BIRTH

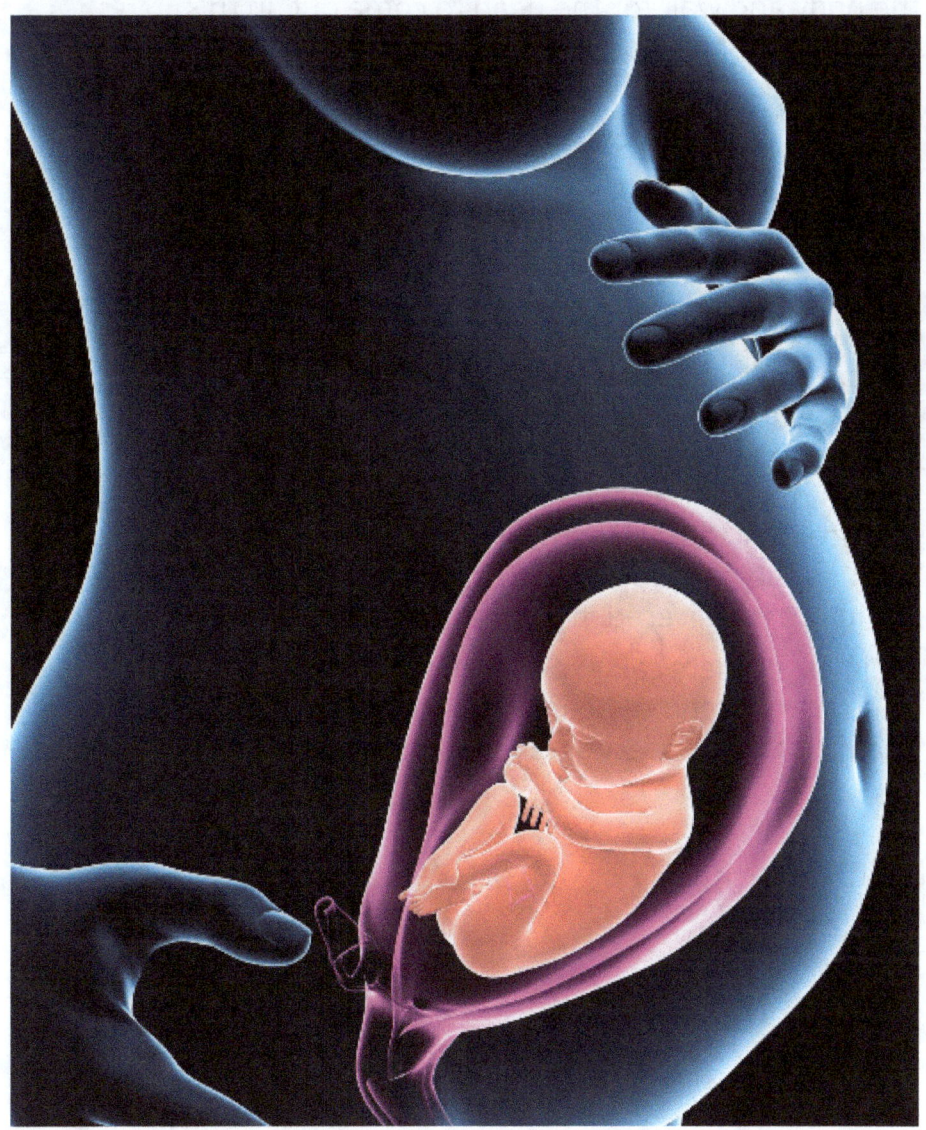

Breech birth

A breech birth happens when a newborn is born with the feet or buttocks first instead of the head. In the case of a breech birth, do not pull the infant; instead, support the body and wait for the head to come out. In this situation, the newborn's weight compresses the umbilical cord, depriving the infant of oxygen. After the delivery, check for breathing and be prepared to perform CPR.

PROLAPSED UMBILICAL CORD

In some instances, the umbilical cord comes out of the vagina before the newborn. This is a life-threatening situation for the newborn because the umbilical cord gets compressed, compromising vital oxygen to the infant. In this situation, the newborn will die within minutes. If this happens, have the mother pull her knees to her chest to help reduce the pressure on the umbilical cord. In this position, the newborn will lack oxygen while moving through the birth canal, so be prepared to give CPR once the infant is delivered. Do not pull on the newborn's body.

At times mothers can experience false labor contractions. Contractions tend to be irregular when this happens and do not get closer together as during true labor.

CHAPTER

WATER-RELATED EMERGENCIES

INTRODUCTION

In this chapter, you will learn how to recognize someone experiencing distress in the water and how to reach and assist them.

LEARNING OBJECTIVES

After reading this chapter, you will be able to:

- Describe how to recognize a water-related emergency
- Describe how to care for someone who experienced a drowning situation
- Describe non-swimmers rescues
- List steps to prevent water-related emergencies

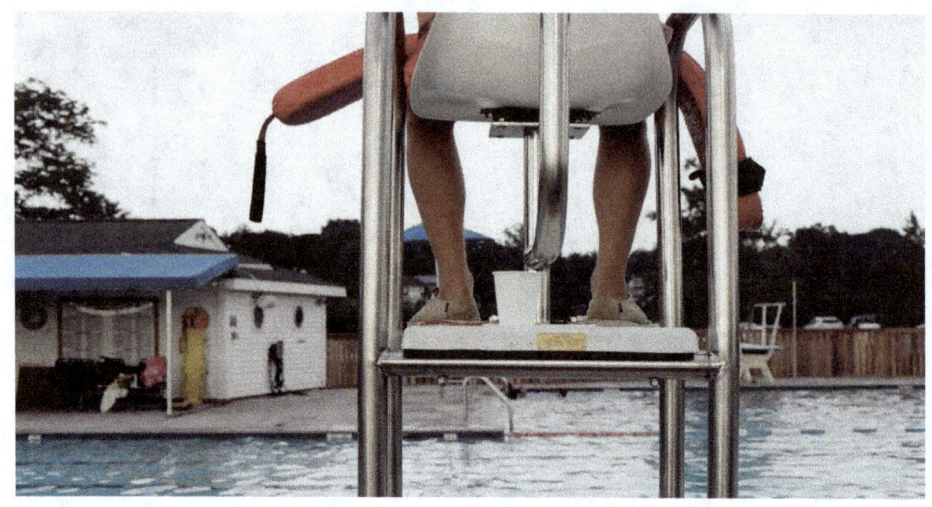

SIGNS OF A WATER-RELATED EMERGENCY

Key signals help determine if a person is experiencing a water-related emergency and what type of emergency it is.

A Distressed Swimmer

Refers to a swimmer who can call for help and float but is too tired to return to shore.

Active Drowning Victim

- The person is unable to go back to shore or call for help
- They may be sinking or at the surface of the water

Passive Drowning Victim

- Limp body or convulsions
- Floating face down or up

GENERAL HELP FOR WATER-RELATED EMERGENCIES

- Unless you have the training to rescue water-related victims, do not swim to the person
- Get a lifeguard if available
- Call for help
- Check the scene. Consider the temperature and depth of the water
- Check for equipment or objects that are available for the rescue
- Talk to the person, and try to have them move towards you
- Use one of the following techniques:

REACHING ASSIST

- Secure yourself to a firm and steady surface, or lay down and extend your arm
- Try to reach out to the person with anything that can extend your reach, such as a pole, a branch, a paddle, or a towel

THROWING ASSIST

- Without entering the water, throw a floating object attached to a line to the drowning person

WADING ASSIST

If the water is shallow enough (below your chest), wear a life jacket if available and reach the person. Use anything to extend your reach toward the person.

CARE FOR AN UNRESPONSIVE PERSON

Use the head-tilt-chin-lift technique and check for breathing. If the person is not breathing, proceed with CPR.

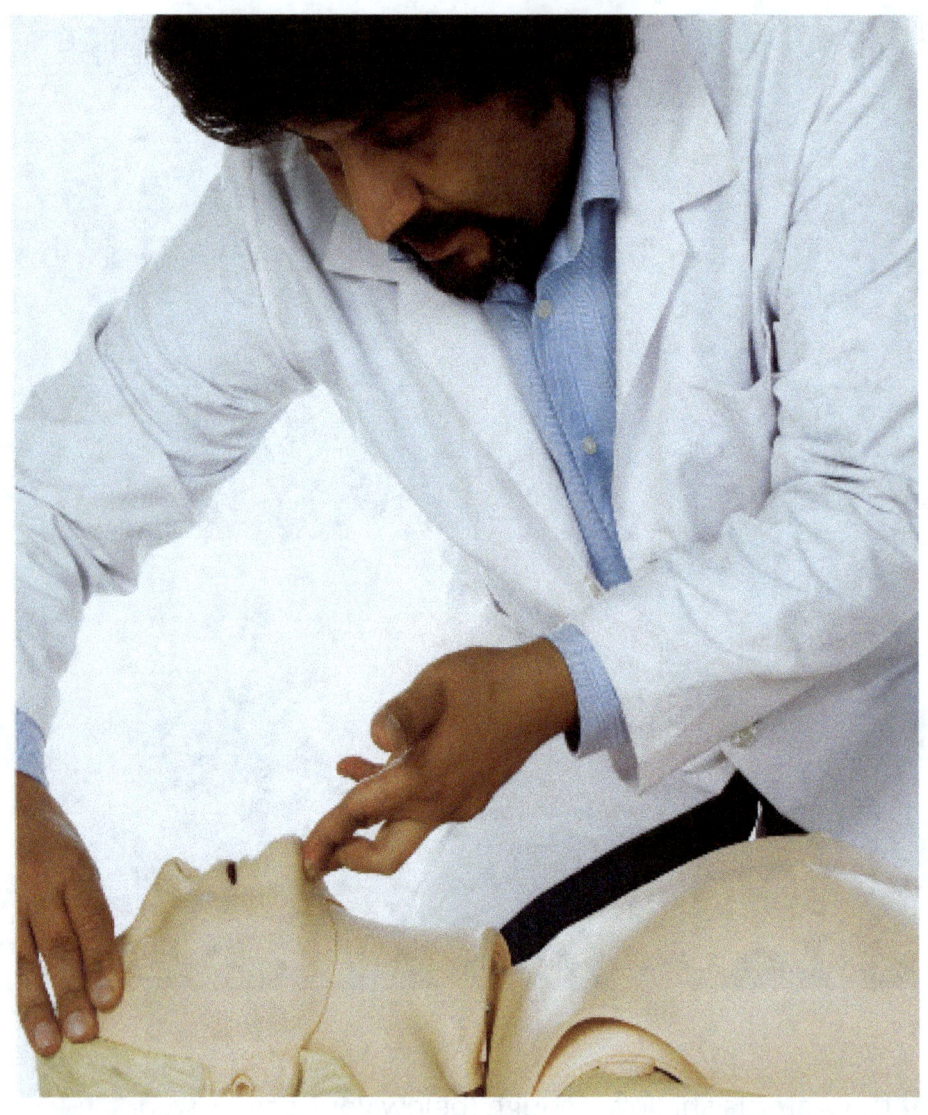

CARE FOR RESPONSIVE PERSON

- Follow the CHECK-CALL-CARE steps
- Call 911

STEPS TO PREVENT WATER-RELATED EMERGENCIES

- Learn how to swim
- Get certified in first aid and CPR
- Keep your CPR training current
- Follow the rules posted
- Always swim with someone else
- Swim in areas supervised by lifeguards
- Find out about hazards, currents, and depths changes
- Do not leave children unattended around water
- Do not drink alcohol when you are going swimming

When providing help in a water-related emergency, ensure you are safe to proceed.

You never know when an emergency may arise. The best safety strategy is always prevention. Learn first aid, and review the skills in this textbook often. You can minimize the risks of chronic diseases by following a healthy diet, and exercising regularly.

Learning first aid and CPR are essential skills that can save lives in an emergency. However, while preparing for emergencies is important, prevention is always the best

strategy. By taking proactive measures, such as being aware of potential hazards, maintaining a healthy lifestyle, and seeking professional medical care when necessary, we can minimize the risks of emergencies occurring in the first place. Prevention is critical, but being prepared with first aid and CPR skills can make all the difference in a life-or-death situation. Stay safe, stay informed, and always be ready to help those in need.

If you enjoyed this book, please support me by leaving a review on Amazon, suggesting it to your friends and family, or offering it as a gift.

To share a review, point your phone's camera at the QR code below and tap the icon on the screen to access the video.

www.ingramcontent.com/pod-product-compliance
Lightning Source LLC
Chambersburg PA
CBHW051647230426
43669CB00013B/2472